Effective Marketing: principles and practice

Jacqueline Bishop

LBP

Published by Liverpool Business Publishing
an imprint of
Liverpool Academic Press

©Jacqueline Bishop 2002

First published in Great Britain by Liverpool Business Publishing.

A CIP catalogue for this book is available from the British Library

ISBN 1 903500 03 6

The right of the author of this work has been asserted by her in accordance with the Copyright, Designs and Patents Act 1988.

Typeset by Bitter & Twisted N. Wales. bitter@cybase.co.uk

Printed and Bound in Great Britain by Lightning Source UK Ltd, Milton Keynes

Effective Marketing: principles and practice

For Phil

Introduction

This book is designed for anyone studying marketing for the first time, either at degree level or as part of a professional qualification. The main principles of marketing are explained clearly and concisely. The academic theory is backed up by examples from industry to illustrate key points.

Each chapter includes a summary of the key terms, to help guide the reader gently through the jargon that so many students find baffling.

Contents

Chapter 3:   The Marketing Environment

Section 2: Analysing and Selecting Markets

Chapter 4:   Marketing Research

Chapter 5:   Consumer Buying Behaviour

Section 4: Marketing Extended

Section 1: An Introduction to Marketing

Chapter 1

The Marketing Concept

Section 1: An introduction to Marketing

What is Marketing?

Marketing is one of those words that is used frequently. We are constantly bombarded by marketing. We hear about companies that market their brands and organisations that market their products and services. Marketing has helped names such as Nike, Proctor and Gamble, Nissan and The Body Shop become familiar to us. Marketing is an area that touches all of our lives. But what is it really about?

Most of us assume that marketing is about advertising. It is. But, simply defining marketing as advertising is restrictive and is certainly not indicative of the full scope of activities with which marketing is concerned. Figure 1.1 gives some indication of the activities that are associated with marketing. You can see that advertising is just one of these activities.

Figure 1.1 The Activities Associated with Marketing

The Purpose of Marketing

Although Figure 1.1 further explains marketing, it does not clarify our understanding the concept of marketing. It does not explain the purpose of marketing.

Marketing is concerned with satisfying customer needs. It is anything that an organisation does in an attempt to satisfy customers. Satisfied customers will return to the organisation in the future and will recommend it to their family and friends and this in turn affects profitability. Put simply, marketing is about customer satisfaction. All of the activities identified in Figure 1.1 are used by organisations in an attempt to achieve customer satisfaction.

Marketing is essential in today's environment. Companies and organisations are facing increased competition and if customers are dissatisfied they will seek satisfaction from competitors.

Marketing Defined

There are many definitions of marketing. The Chartered Institute of Marketing (CIM) defines it as 'the management process responsible for identifying, anticipating and satisfying customers profitably.'

This definition indicates that marketing is actually a process that can be followed. It is, but merely following a process will not ensure customer satisfaction. The whole purpose of an organisation should be geared toward customer satisfaction. We will look at marketing processes throughout this book but you should bear in mind that marketing is an organisational culture or philosophy rather than a procedure or process.

Kotler defines marketing as 'a societal process by which individuals and groups obtain what they need and want through creating, offering, and freely exchanging products and services of value to others.'

This definition brings in the concept of exchange. As consumers, we exchange money for goods and services. The goods satisfy our needs and wants. The money satisfies the company's need for profitability. So marketing is the basis of profitability for many organisations. Figure 1.2 overviews the exchange process. The arrows indicate that each party has something of value to exchange.

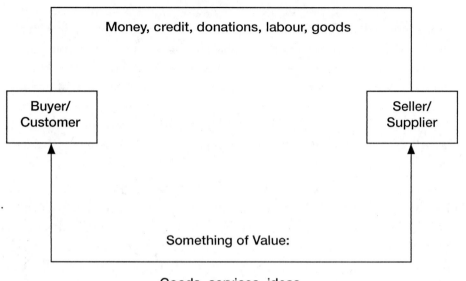

Figure 1.2 The Concept of Marketing (adapted from Dibb et al)

Figure 1.2 indicates that marketing is not solely the domain of profit-making organisations. People can offer donations to charities which in turn donate goods to beneficiaries. Workers offer labour to government organisations who in turn provide services to the general public. Marketing is concerned with both profit-making and non-profit-making organisations. In the case of not-for-profit organisations, marketing is a means to achieve strategic objectives.

These definitions widen our understanding of marketing. But at the basis of all marketing activities is the objective of customer satisfaction.

Organisational Philosophies

As we mentioned earlier, marketing is more than a process. It is an organisational philosophy or culture, the governing philosophy for the whole organisation.   In today's competitive world it might seem improbable that some organisations do not put customers at the heart of their planning, but other approaches to business are still apparent.

Some companies are **production orientated**. Their sole purpose is to produce goods of optimum quality and cost. We are not arguing that quality and cost control are not essential elements of any organisation but that, if this philosophy is pursued, an organisation cannot survive. If the company were marketing orientated, it would first identify its customers' needs and wants and then produce goods at optimum quality and cost that satisfied those needs. The difference here is that customers want the goods. Simply producing goods with no knowledge of customers' needs will be unsuccessful.

Another organisational philosophy is **sales orientation**. This type of philosophy focuses on selling and promotion as a means to success. The belief here is that a good sales force can sell anything. Again, selling and promotion are essential activities for many organisations but an organisation that concentrates solely on these activities will fail. If the company were marketing orientated, sales and promotion would help with selling goods but potential customers would already have a need or want for the goods being sold. You've probably heard the term 'hard sell'. It is a concept that has been typically associated with double glazing sales people where the customer is pressured into signing on the dotted line. Yes, the sale is achieved but the customer may be dissatisfied and will warn friends and family to avoid the company in question. In turn, the long-term profitability of the company is questionable.

Marketing orientation is the philosophy that puts the customer at the heart of everything the organisation does. Figure 3.1 displays the distinction between marketing orientation and selling/production orientation. You can see from this Figure that the key concern for the marketing orientated organisation is customer needs. Theodore Levitt distinguishes these orientations well: 'Selling focuses on the needs of the seller; marketing on the needs of the buyer'.

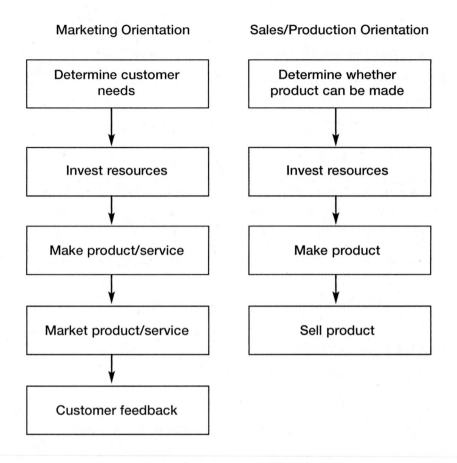

Figure 1.3 Organisational Philosophies

An organisation that is marketing orientated finds out, through research, what its customers want. It then invests time and money to produce the goods and services that will satisfy these customer wants. However, this is not enough. The marketing orientated organisation will also:

◆ continually seek feedback from customers about products and services so that it can improve those products and services or create new ones that better satisfy customer wants

◆ communicate the importance of marketing throughout the organisation; all staff will be trained in the importance of achieving customer satisfaction

attempt to build relationships with key customers

◆ recognise the strategic importance of marketing and ensure the marketing is represented at board level

develop and implement a well-researched marketing plan

develop a mission statement that highlights customer satisfaction as the focus for the entire organisation; for example, supermarket chain Tesco states that its core purpose or mission is 'to create value for customers to earn their lifetime loyalty'.

This initial discussion might indicate that marketing is an expensive process, but, there are many benefits to be gained. An organisation that adopts a marketing orientation will:

achieve long-term survival

increase profitability

increase customer loyalty

build relationships with customers and suppliers

◆ benefit from word of mouth

◆ plan for changes in the environment

identify customer trends

◆ invest in new product development

gain advantage over its competitors.

Customer Needs and Wants

Throughout this chapter we have continually referred to customer needs and wants. It is customers with similar needs and wants that comprise a market.

Needs and wants are the driving forces that impel a person towards certain objectives - usually the satisfaction of the need or want. A need is a necessity. For example, if you were hungry, you would have a need for food. If you were cold, you would have a need for clothing or heat. Wants are the objects or things that satisfy needs. For example, you may want a Mars Bar to satisfy your need for food. It is these needs and wants that organisations attempt to satisfy.

This process of satisfaction is not a straightforward as it appears. Many companies such as McDonald's, Nestle and Heinz offer products that satisfy the need for food. As the potential customer, you can select products from any of these companies to satisfy your need. Again, this highlights the competitive situation in the market place.

Furthermore, just because you have a need or want, it does not necessarily follow that you are part of the market. For example, you may need transportation, but you may want a new Porsche. However, to form part of the market for a Porsche, you would have to earn a substantial salary. Markets are formed of those people with similar needs and wants who also have the ability to pay.

Summary

This chapter has provided a brief introduction to marketing. You should recognise that marketing is concerned with any activities that an organisation performs in an attempt to satisfy its customers.

Marketing is more than a process, it is a culture, a philosophy. The company that puts customers at the heart of all its operations will achieve its objectives.

Review Questions

1. Define marketing.
2. What are the activities that are typically associated with marketing?
3. What is the purpose of marketing?
4. What does sales orientation mean?

5. What are the disadvantages of sales orientation and production orientation?

6. What are the benefits of marketing orientation?

7. What are needs?

8. What are wants?

9. What is a market?

Discussion Questions

1. Identify two companies that you consider to be marketing-orientated.

   What actions have these companies taken recently that demonstrate a marketing orientation?

2. Why is marketing necessary in today's society?

3. Do the following goods satisfy needs or wants:

   -a Mars Bar?

   -a pair of Levi jeans?

   -a Ford Mondeo?

4. 'Marketing is unnecessary in not-for-profit organisations'. Discuss.

5. How can an organisation ensure a marketing orientation is developed?

Key Terms

Customers	Place	Sales orientation
Exchange	Price	Satisfaction
Market	Product	Want
Marketing	Production	
Marketing orientation	orientation	
Need	Promotion	
Organisation	Research	
philosophies		

Chapter 2
The Marketing Planning Process

Introduction

In this chapter we move on to look at the marketing planning process. This is the part of marketing that is usually managed by the marketing department. However, marketing is not an isolated function. The marketing plan must be communicated and co-ordinated throughout the organisation.

Why Plan?

Planning improves the chance of success and reduces the risk of failure for an organisation. Planning drives an organisation forward by allocating resources so that goals can be achieved. Planning is also important for staff. They need to understand where the organisation is heading if they are to feel a sense of purpose.

Although essential, planning does take time and money. Marketing planning should be a continuous process and managers need to invest their time in developing it. Not surprisingly, many organisations fail to develop a marketing plan. There are obvious risks associated with this. For instance, competitors might identify opportunities for new products or services or they might spot a change in customer needs and wants. The organisation that does not constantly monitor and plan for change will, eventually, fail.

The Marketing Planning Process

Figure 2.1 details the stages in the marketing planning process. We will discuss each one in some depth in this chapter. You should understand this process because each subsequent chapter of this book is part of the planning process.

The result of the planning process is the marketing plan. It is important that each stage of the process is followed so that the resulting plan is realistic and achievable.

The marketing plan is strategic; it is long-term. In business terms, a long-term or strategic plan is one that looks three to five years ahead. An organisation should take a strategic view when planning otherwise it will react to change rather than anticipate change before it occurs. The fact that the marketing plan is strategic highlights the importance of following each stage of the planning process.

Corporate Objectives

The purpose of any organisation is to achieve the overall corporate objectives. Corporate objectives describe the desired goals of the company and are usually concerned with profits, sales, resources, return on investment and share price. Marketing plays a part in achieving the corporate objectives. The rest of the planning process highlighted in Figure 2.1 is concerned with achieving the overall goals of the organisation.

The other functions within an organisation also work towards achieving corporate objectives. Figure 2.2 shows how each function has a role to play in achieving corporate objectives. Therefore, it is essential that each function co-ordinates and communicates its plans and activities throughout the organisation. It is only through co-ordination that corporate objectives can be achieved.

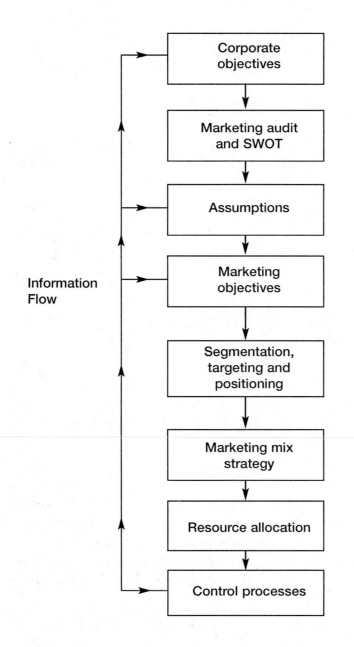

Figure 2.1 The Marketing Planning Process

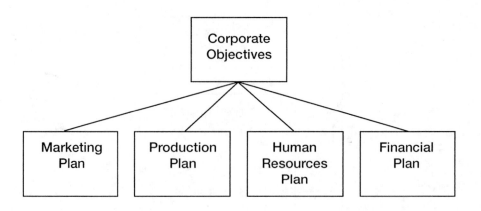

Figure 2.2 Relationship of Functional Plans to Corporate Objectives

The Marketing Audit, SWOT Analysis and Assumptions

Once the corporate objectives have been developed a marketing audit should be performed. Performing an audit involves extensive information gathering to assess the current situation of the company and the environment in which it operates. According to Adcock *et al*, it has four major components. These are:

1. **The external/macro environment:** this includes macro factors which are essentially uncontrollable. These are often referred to as the **PEST** factors – Political/legal, Economic, Social and Technological. These macro factors impact on everything an organisation does. Consider how demand for goods and services increases when the UK has a strong economy. The effects of the macro environment are discussed in detail in Chapter 3 of this book.

2. **The stakeholder system/micro environment:** stakeholders include customers, competitors, the general public, distributors such as wholesalers and retailers, suppliers, employees, banks and shareholders. Chapter 3 will discuss the influence of stakeholders on the organisation.

3. **The organisation's markets:** an audit of the markets in which the organisation operates and its performance within these markets is essential. Knowledge of the size of the market, market trends and the organisation's ability to meet the needs of the market are required.

4. **The organisation itself:** this includes a review of the resources and skills as well as the systems and process that operate within an organisation.

Only by gathering the above information can an organisation hope to develop realistic marketing objectives. It is this information that forms the basis of the **SWOT** analysis.

The SWOT (Strengths, Weaknesses, Opportunities and Threats) analysis is an aid to objective setting. You can see from Figure 2.3 that strengths and weaknesses are internal to the organisation, while opportunities and threats are external to the organisation. While the audit is a straightforward information gathering exercise, the SWOT analysis gives meaning to the information. For example, during the audit a company may gain information that the size of the market is declining and that several competitors intend to stop producing goods to satisfy that market. During the analysis stage, it must be decided whether this information is an opportunity or threat. It may be an opportunity because competitors are leaving the market. Alternatively, it may be a threat because the market is declining. A decision should be taken at this stage.

Figure 2.3 The SWOT Analysis

The entire SWOT analysis forms the basis for setting marketing objectives. But, before objectives are developed, assumptions must be made.

Assumptions are educated guesses or forecasts about some of the factors that may affect the marketing plan. These factors might include assumptions about market growth rates, government policy, competitor activity, etc. Obviously, no organisation can see into the future, therefore assumptions are essential if the planning process is to continue.

Marketing Objectives

Marketing objectives guide the whole operation of the marketing function. The purpose of marketing objectives is to achieve the corporate objectives (see Figure 2.2). Information required for setting marketing objectives has already been gathered during the audit stage and analysed during the SWOT stage of the planning process. Along with this information, McDonald suggests the use of the Ansoff matrix (see Figure 2.4). The Ansoff matrix identifies four possible strategic options for any company: penetration, product development, market development and/or diversification.

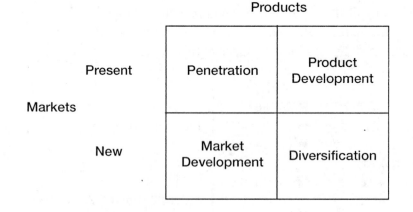

Figure 2.4 The Ansoff Matrix

From the Ansoff matrix, you can see that any organisation is concerned with products (or services) and the markets it sells to. Each strategic option offers direction to the entire marketing function.

Penetration: this means that an organisation will strive to increase its market share by selling more of its present products. This objective might be achieved through advertising and promotional activities, increasing the distribution of products, or by reducing prices. This is perhaps the least risky option as the company has a good level of knowledge of both its customers and the products it is already selling.

Marketing development: the organisation seeks to identify new markets (customers) for its present products. For instance, a British organisation might look to international markets to identify new customers for its products. Alternatively, new customers groups could be sought. Think about the drink Lucozade. Traditionally, it was sold as a drink for the ill. Now the company targets the product at consumers who play sports.

Product development: here, the organisation attempts to create new products for present customers. By doing this, customers are encouraged to remain loyal. The Body Shop is an example of a company that pursues this strategy. The Body Shop continually introduces new products to its range.

Diversification: this is perhaps the riskiest strategy as in means that the organisation seeks to develop new products for new markets.

To select the appropriate marketing objectives from the strategic options discussed above, the organisation should consider the corporate objectives, information gathered during the audit and SWOT analysis, market trends and competitors' strategy.

Drucker states that objectives must be:

◆ Derived from 'what our business is, what it will be and what it should be'. Objectives are the fundamental strategy of the business.

◆ Capable of being converted into specific targets, projects and tasks.

◆ Selective so that they make possible the best allocation of resources.

◆ Multiple rather than single. A business requires a variety of objectives.

As with corporate and other functional objectives, marketing objectives should be SMARTER:

◆ **S**pecific: state exactly what the target is

◆ **M**easurable: establish a form of measure (either qualitative or quantitative)

◆ **A**ttainable: with the resources that are available

◆ **R**ealistic: in terms of the market and the competition

◆ **T**ime-based: a specific date when they will be achieved

◆ **E**valuated: constantly throughout the planning cycle in case the

◆ **R**eviewed: market, competitive or economic situation changes

The SMARTER acronym provides a simple approach to objective setting. For instance, an organisation wishing to further penetrate its market might state that it wishes to 'increase market share by ten per cent'. This objective is not SMARTER. It is not time-based and so effective evaluation and review is impossible. An example of a SMARTER objective might be: 'We will achieve a ten per cent increase in market share by 31 December 2001'.

Segmentation, Targeting and Positioning

Before any organisation can work towards its objectives, it must identify its customers – whether they be existing or potential customers. Remember, marketing is concerned with customer satisfaction. It is through customer satisfaction that objectives are achieved. Therefore, a thorough understanding of customers is required.

It is unusual for an organisation to attempt to satisfy everyone. Most organisations have a specific group or segment of the market that they attempt to satisfy. For instance, Nike's customers are interested in sport, Sony's customers are interested in music and TV and Dell's customers need computers. An organisation needs to understand its customer groups. Chapter 7 discusses the concept of segmentation, targeting and positioning in some detail.

Marketing Mix Strategy

The marketing mix is the basis of most marketing activity. It is the marketer's tool box. The elements of the marketing mix are used strategically and tactically to achieve the marketing objectives and, therefore, the overall corporate objectives.

The marketing mix is also referred to as the 4 Ps – a mnemonic first used by McCarthy. The 4 Ps are a set of elements over which the organisation has full control. They are:

Product: this is the products or services that an organisation offers to its customers. Take a computer, for example. This product consists of a screen, a keyboard and a hard drive, as well as all the bits that make up these items. Usually, this product also includes software and guarantees. Chapter 8 discusses the concept of the product in some detail.

Price: this is the amount of money customers must exchange for the product or service. For instance, the price of a computer might be £999.00. Chapter 9 addresses pricing issues. Price is a key element of the marketing mix as it generates income for the organisation. All other elements of the mix incur costs. Therefore, the pricing decision is critical to the success of an organisation.

Place: another word for place is distribution; how the products or services are actually made available to customers. Customers may visit a retailer to purchase their computer or alternatively they might order it direct from the manufacturer. Chapter 10 looks at distribution alternatives.

Promotion: this involves communication with potential customers to encourage them to buy the product or service. Promotion of a computer might include advertising, mailshots, sponsorship and personal selling within the retail outlet. Promotion is discussed in Chapter 11.

The marketing mix is the basis of all marketing strategy and must be understood. It is the marketing mix which encourages customers to spend money. Each element is managed to form a total image and to satisfy the needs and wants of potential customers. For example, take Coca-Cola. It obviously satisfies thirst. The product is in a red and white can containing liquid and flavourings, it is sold at a relatively low price, distributed world-wide and constantly promoted in mass media.

Marketing mix decisions are complex. There are an enormous amount of alternatives to be considered within each element of the mix. This book discusses the alternatives in some detail. In reality, the marketing manager will make mix decisions based on the target customer, the marketing objectives and the corporate objectives.

Chapter 12 deals with the marketing mix for services. Along with the traditional 4 Ps, another 3 Ps should be considered because of the nature of services marketing.

In recent years, the concept of the 4 Ps has been criticised. Professor Don Schultz says that, because of the power of the modern consumer and the increasingly competitive environment, a better approach to marketing strategy is the 4 R approach:

- ◆ **Relevance:** because of the enormous number of alternatives available to customers to satisfy needs and wants, the marketer must ensure that the products and services being offered are relevant to customers.

- ◆ **Response:** organisations should learn to listen and respond to the desires and needs of customers.

- ◆ **Relationships:** rather than managing the marketing mix, organisations and marketers should be concerned with managing the customer relationship. It costs far more to attract new customers than to retain and satisfy existing customers by encouraging them to repeat purchase. And lost customers are hard to win back.

- ◆ **Returns:** The 4 P approach is concerned with the organisation's offering to customers. Instead, the organisation should be concerned with the returns it generates in terms of income and profit.

The 4 R approach is again geared towards customer satisfaction and achievement of organisational goals. However, most marketers still rely on the 4 P approach to managing marketing strategy.

Resource Allocation

Once the marketing mix decisions have been taken, resources must be allocated to them. This is not a straightforward allocation of money. Resources include human resources, time and production, materials, etc.

To implement the marketing mix strategy, the marketing planner might:

◆ establish full resource requirements

◆ establish currently available resources

◆ decide whether current resources are sufficient to pursue the marketing mix strategy and take appropriate action

◆ allocate resources

Control Process

Resources are costly for the organisation. If resources are not used effectively and efficiently, an organisation may not survive. Effective use of resources means that the marketing/corporate objectives are achieved. Efficient use of resources means that the marketing/corporate objectives are achieved at low cost.

So, simply allocating resources is insufficient. The entire marketing planning process must be controlled. Control means that strategies are monitored and evaluated to ensure they are meeting the marketing/corporate objectives within the resource allocation.

To do this, an organisation might measure and evaluate:

◆ sales levels

◆ market share

◆   costs

◆   profits

◆   customer opinions/attitudes to organisation and its products

◆   competitor profits/market share.

Summary

This chapter has provided an overview of the marketing planning process. Each stage is crucial if the organisation wishes to achieve customer satisfaction over a period of time.

The remainder of this book relates to this planning process. You will see that each stage in planning involves making decisions about a wide range of variables. Marketing is a strategic process, and, if the organisation is to be marketing orientated, then a marketing plan is essential. It should be communicated throughout the entire organisation.

Review Questions

1. Why is marketing planning essential?
2. What are the stages in the marketing planning process?
3. How do marketing objectives relate to corporate objectives?
4. What is the purpose of the marketing audit?
5. Explain the Ansoff matrix.
6. What are the elements of the marketing mix?
7. What is the purpose of the marketing mix?
8. Explain the concept of 'control' within the planning process.

Discussion Questions

1. 'Organisations can exist without a formalised planning process'. Discuss.

2. Is it possible for one organisation to pursue each strategic option identified in the Ansoff matrix simultaneously?   Explain your answer.

3. Explain how the marketing mix is used for each of the following products:

   - Porsche cars

   - Dell computers

   - Digital TV.

4. 'The marketing plan is only as important as the financial plan, the HR plan and the production plan'. Discuss

Key Terms

4 Ps	Marketing development	Product development
4 Rs	Marketing mix	Resource
Ansoff matrix	Marketing objectives	Segmentation
Assumptions	Objectives	Strategy
Control	Penetration	SWOT analysis
Diversification	Planning	Targeting
Functional objectives	Positioning	The planning process
Marketing audit		

Chapter 3
The External Environment

Introduction

Chapter 2 highlighted the fact that organisations do not operate in a vacuum. They are affected by external factors and forces that are essentially uncontrollable. These external factors must be monitored because they present both opportunities and threats to an organisation.

During the audit stage of the marketing planning process, an organisation will gather as much information as possible about the external environment. However, this is insufficient. Constant monitoring is necessary because the external environment is constantly changing. Figure 3.1 displays the factors of the external environment that affect the organisation and its marketing plan.

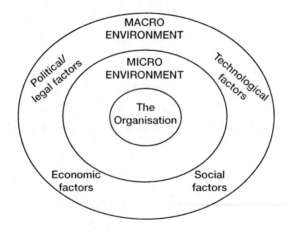

Figure 3.1   The External Environment

The Macro Environment

You can see from Figure 3.1 that the macro environment consists of political/legal factors, economic factors, social factors and technological factors. For ease, these factors are often referred to as the PEST factors. Organisations usually have no control over these factors but if they are ignored the organisation has little chance of success. Think about companies that made typewriters. Typewriters are no longer in demand because technology has improved and PCs are now the norm. A company that failed to see this trend and continued to produce typewriters would no longer be commercially successful.

Political/Legal Factors

Marketing decisions are strongly influenced by political/legal factors. Politically, organisations are influenced by government policy on expenditure, competition, taxation and, in Britain, European policy. Any change in government policy needs to be understood if an organisation is to be successful.

For instance, if the government increases corporation tax, profits may suffer. In turn, shareholders may not be satisfied with the returns on their investment. In this case, an organisation may have to consider new strategies to increase profitability. In marketing terms, this may result in price increases or a reduction in promotional activity.

If the government increases income tax, the average consumer may have less money to spend. Again, the result of this may be a decrease in profits for an organisation. To increase profits, the organisation may consider a change in the make-up of the product so that less costs are incurred. In turn, the selling price could be lowered.

You can see from these two examples that political factors can affect corporate objectives, marketing objectives and marketing strategies (the marketing mix).

Every organisation operates within a legal system. Most activities that an organisation performs will be within the law. However, laws are constantly changing. In Britain, because of our membership of the EU, we must also be aware of European legislation.

Laws that have a direct impact on business activity include the Sale of Goods Act, the Supply of Goods and Services Act, the Consumer Protection Act and the Consumer Credit Act. Although organisations have the power to interpret these laws, there are many regulatory bodies that ensure the laws are enforced. For example:

◆ The Department for Trade and Industry (DTI) controls industrial and commercial policy, competition and investor and consumer protection.

◆ The Department of the Environment and the Regions (DETR) controls policies for planning and regional development.

When making marketing mix decisions, the marketer must be aware of the law.

Economic Factors

Related to political factors is the state of the economy. This has a direct impact on the quantity of goods demanded and the prices at which they can be sold. Richard Lynch in *Corporate Strategy* states that the following economic factors are relevant to an organisation:

Growth: if the economy is growing, it is much easier for an organisation to grow and expand. On the other hand, if economic decline is likely, an organisation might concentrate on maintaining its current business. You've probably witnessed the economy in a state of decline and boom. During boom times consumers are likely to spend more freely, while during decline they are likely to be more prudent. This obviously affects marketing strategies.

Interest rates: this can have an affect on both the organisation and its customers. Many organisations rely on financial assistance in the form of loans, etc. High interest rates will increase the cost of loans and so decrease profitability. Likewise, high interest rates affect consumer spending power meaning they have less disposable income and, therefore, demand less goods.

Inflation: this refers to any rises in price levels. If consumer income rises at the same rate of inflation, then it has little overall effect. However if consumer income/wages do not increase with inflation, they have less money to spend on goods and services.

Unemployment: again, if unemployment levels are high, consumer spending is usually lower. Fewer goods are demanded. This affects the product and pricing policy of an organisation.

The discussion of economic factors constantly refers to consumers. It is important to understand that these factors also impact on organisations that sell to other organisations, otherwise known as business-to-business marketing. Demand for business and industrial goods is derived from ultimate consumer demand. So the industrial marketer should also monitor economic factors and their impact on the ultimate consumer.

Social Factors

This part of the macro environment is formed of demographics and cultural factors.

Demography is concerned with the population and its make-up. Marketers are concerned with the population as it is groups of people that make up the market for a product or service.

The UK has a population of approximately 59 million people. Figure 3.2 provides an overview of how the population is broken down. You can see from this figure that 25-29 year olds and 30-34 year olds are the largest sectors of the UK population. This type of information is useful for marketers because it provides an indication of the potential size of their market. For example, Next sells clothes for women between the ages of 25 to 39.

Years of Age	Total '000s	%
0-4	3,763.4	6.4
5-9	3,905.3	6.6
10-14	3,689.6	6.3
15-19	3,522.3	6.0
20-24	3,802.8	6.5
25-29	4,577.6	7.8
30-34	4,842.6	8.2
35-39	4,289.3	7.3
40-44	3,803.6	6.5
45-49	4,129.7	7.0
50-54	3,495.9	5.9
55-59	2,986.4	5.1
60-64	2,772.2	4.7
65-69	2,646.3	4.5
70-74	2,412.0	4.1
75-79	1,823.7	3.1
80-84	1,301.6	2.2
85+	1,067.2	1.8

Figure 3.2   The UK Population   (Source: Marketing Pocket Book 1998)

It is interesting to note that Britain has an ageing population. Figure 3.2 shows that almost 32% of the population is over 50. Many companies have recognised this growth and sell products and services that are aimed at people over 50. For instance, Saga Holidays directly targets this market.

The ageing population may be attributed to better medicine and medical services, healthier eating and generally healthier lifestyles. It is estimated that there will be over 40,000 people aged 100 and over in the UK by 2036. This is a market that continues to grow.

Marketers will carefully monitor population trends to ensure there is a sufficient market for their goods. This information can be made more useful by measuring income distribution and spending habits of each of the age categories.

Culture is concerned with the norms of a society. Culture constantly evolves and does change over time. Here are some interesting facts about the UK population:

72% of women are now in paid employment

62% of couples with children have both parents working

approximately 40% of births are outside marriage

men work an average of approximately 46 hours per week

approximately 30% of households have no savings

life expectancy for men is 75 years of age, 80 for women

the average weekly spend on food is £59.00.

Source: Social Trends 30

You can see that social information is important to any organisation. The fact that more women are working may mean that there is increased demand for home help. The fact that 40% of births are outside of marriage indicates that this is perhaps becoming a social norm. Because almost a third of households have little or no savings, perhaps this is a relatively untapped market.

Social and demographic trends indicate to organisations the levels and types of demand that will exist.

Technological Factors

Technology is developing at a phenomenal pace. Most of us have probably used the internet, or at least heard of it. Organisations must keep up with the pace of technological change.

Technology can be used by an organisation to gain competitive advantage. It is used to improve processes and minimise cost throughout an organisation. If an organisation does not monitor technological developments, it may be left behind by its competitors.

In fact many new industries and organisations have emerged because of technological developments. For example, advanced telecommunications has led to digital televisions, on-line banking and e-tailing (retailers that sell their goods on the internet).

The internet is a beneficial tool for the marketer. The marketer can access information in any field in a relatively quick and cheap way. Additionally, the internet can be used to keep abreast of new technological developments. According to Bickerton, Bickerton and Pardes, the internet can aid the marketer to keep abreast of technological developments in three ways:

1. It provides access to up-to-date information about technological developments. IT companies provide information about their services and will sometimes answer questions that organisations may have about IT.

2. It provides access to information about the technologies competitors are using. Companies often promote themselves on the web and will give indication of the type of technology they are using.

3. It can be used to investigate and gauge customers' reaction to and need for new technology. Many companies use the internet as a way to test their new products and services.

The Micro Environment

Figure 3.1 indicates that, as well as the macro environment, organisations are influenced by the micro environment. Figure 3.3 provides an overview of the members of the micro environment. Many theorists also term this the stakeholder system. Like the macro environment, the micro environment must be constantly monitored (especially during the audit stage of the planning process). This environment presents both opportunities and threats to an organisation. It is interesting to note that, unlike the macro environment, the members of the micro environment are closer to an organisation. In other words, the organisation has some direct contact with these members. Even though micro environment members are essentially uncontrollable, the organisation can influence them directly.

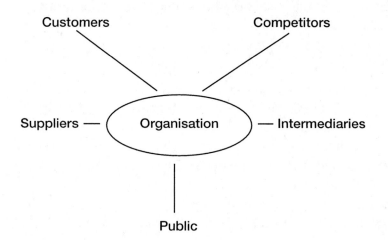

Figure 3.3 The Micro Environment

Customers

Marketing is concerned with customer satisfaction – it is the key to marketing orientation. Because of this, an organisation must identify and understand its customers.

Think back to the CIM definition of marketing: 'The management process for identifying, anticipating and satisfying customer needs at a profit'.

To identify and anticipate the needs of customers, an organisation should gather information about them. The information required might include such facts as:

- ◆ who they are
- ◆ how much they have to spend
- ◆ why they buy products
- ◆ what products they are likely to buy
- ◆ from whom they are likely to buy
- ◆ where they are located.

In fact, the more information gathered about customers, the more likely an organisation is to be able to satisfy them. Customer knowledge will provide the organisation with the information needed to develop a marketing mix that will satisfy customer needs.

The importance of the customer can never be underestimated. Customers are the basis of effective marketing. Customers are part of the micro environment and they cannot be controlled. However, marketers have the ability to influence customers through the goods and services they provide, through the prices they charge, by making the goods and services available and by communicating and promoting effectively so that customers understand their offerings - in other words, through effective use of the marketing mix. Often, organisations attempt to build long-term relationships with their customers so that customers remain loyal.

Because customer knowledge, understanding and satisfaction is key to marketing, this area will be dealt with is some detail in later chapters of this book. Chapter 4 explains the research techniques that might be used to gather information about customers (and other factors). Chapters 5 and 6 explain buyer behaviour in some detail.

Internet usage is a technological development, and with PC ownership a growing social trend, internet shopping is becoming more commonplace. To respond to this growing trend many companies now offer websites where customers can view products on offer.

Competitors

Customer satisfaction is key to marketing but, unfortunately, simply satisfying customers is insufficient. There are many organisations that offer similar products and services that are directly competing with one another. Competition is continually increasing especially because the global market place is now a reality. Companies in the UK now compete with companies from all over the world. The customer will usually buy from the organisation that best satisfies his or her needs. Because of this, the organisation should monitor the competitive environment and competitors' offerings.

If you want to buy a PC for home or office, you might consider the brand, the price, the features of the PC, the software packages and the after-sales guarantees. Some of these factors may be more important to you than others and so you will buy from the company that best matches your requirements. Many companies will be competing for your money.

Michael Porter's Five Forces model (displayed in Figure 3.4) is a useful tool for an organisation wishing to examine its competitive environment. By examining each of the five forces illustrated in the model, the organisation can gain an insight into the opportunities and threats that might exist within an industry.

Before using this model, organisations need to understand who their competitors are. In the case of a clothing retailer such as Next, competition is not simply from other clothing retailers. Next might compete directly with department stores, supermarkets (that are increasingly offering clothing), mail-order firms and organisations that sell clothing over the internet.

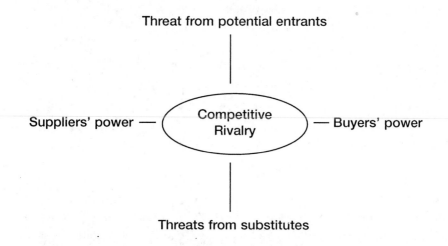

Threat from potential entrants

Suppliers' power — Competitive Rivalry — Buyers' power

Threats from substitutes

Figure 3.4 Porter's Five Forces Model

Competitive rivalry: we know that organisations continually strive to produce new products and services to better meet the needs of their customers. Competitive rivalry will be high when there are many competitors that offer similar or 'me-too' products. If this is the case, companies may compete on price and promotion and may be aggressive towards each other.

Look at the UK food retailing industry. The four biggest food retailers in Britain are Tesco, Sainsbury's, Asda and Safeway. The degree of rivalry among these retailers is high. We see constant price offers and a high level of advertising to attract consumers to their stores.

Threat from potential entrants: alongside existing competition, an organisation should monitor whether new entrants to a market are likely. Any new entrant can have a large impact on the market. The new company may introduce new strategies that better satisfy customer needs. In the UK, Wal-Mart has recently purchased the Asda chain of supermarkets. The UK retailers are likely to be closely monitoring the actions of this new competitor.

Buyer's power: to be able to sell or manufacture goods, most organisations must buy from other organisations. Using our example of food retailers, these companies buy from suppliers such as Heinz, Proctor and Gamble and Coca-Cola. The final selling price is somewhat dependant on the prices at which the retailer purchases its goods from the suppliers.

Because of their power and market share, Tesco, Sainsbury's, Asda and Safeway are likely to have a high level of bargaining power. They buy in bulk and have the ability to negotiate pricing and delivery terms. Therefore, their buying power is strong.

Supplier's power: suppliers are likely to be in a strong position if buyers(retailers) are smaller with less ability to bulk buy. Smaller retailers such as corner shops often have to accept the selling prices that suppliers offer. These increased prices are, in turn, passed on to the consumer.

Threat of substitutes: substitute products are those products that satisfy similar needs and wants. An example of a substitute is an artificial sweetener instead of sugar or margarine instead of butter. Again, the level of substitutes available means that there is more competition in the market. To retain its customers, an organisation may have to promote more, reduce its prices or offer alternative means of distribution for its products.

By using Porter's Five Forces model, organisations can assess their position relative to their customers, suppliers and competitors. It is a tool that can aid marketing mix decisions so that the organisation can gain competitive advantage.

Suppliers

We have already mentioned the importance of suppliers in this chapter. In order to satisfy its customers, an organisation needs to ensure that it maintains a reliable supplier base.

The concept of relationship marketing is constantly being researched. One important relationship an organisation has is with its suppliers, especially if supplier power is high. By building a relationship, perhaps contractually, organisations may be able to ensure the continuity of supply so that they in turn can satisfy their own customers. Building a relationship with suppliers therefore helps an organisation to gain competitive advantage.

Supplier power is strong (see Figure 3.4) when:

- ◆ there is a limited number of suppliers
- ◆ there is a large number of buyers
- ◆ there is a lack of substitutes in the market place
- ◆ the supplier's customers are of little importance to the supplier.

Intermediaries

Many organisations do not sell to the consumer. They sell to other businesses or intermediaries. For instance, Coca-Cola sells its products to retailers (intermediaries). In this case, Coca-Cola is somewhat reliant on intermediaries for the distribution of its products. Again, building relationships with intermediaries is important to ensure that products are sold.

The use of intermediaries should not be confused with business-to-business marketing. In business-to-business marketing, the organisation sells its products and services to another business without the purpose of resale. BT operates in the business-to-business arena (as well as the consumer market). It sells telecommunications systems to individual companies. Brick producers sell to building companies.

Publics

Apart from those already mentioned, another important micro environmental factor is the organisation's publics. Publics are any groups that have an interest in the organisation. Figure 3.5 indicates the types of publics that exist. Although publics may not be customers, they have a direct impact on the success of the organisation. Consider how the media can impact on your view of various organisations.

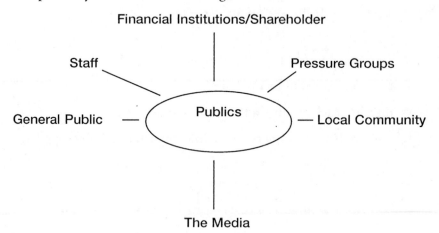

Figure 3.5 The Publics of an Organisation

Staff are a key element for any organisation. It is staff that face customers. It is staff that produce goods and services. They may help to come up with new product ideas. A motivated workforce is productive and beneficial to any organisation.

Marketers recognise the importance of staff in their pursuit of customer satisfaction. Because of this, the concept of internal marketing has come to the fore. Internal marketing regards employees as another key customer of the business. It is concerned with satisfaction of internal customers. In other words, staff satisfaction. If staff are satisfied by their jobs, their salaries and their working conditions, they are likely to perform better. On the other hand, a dissatisfied member of staff may result in loss of business for an organisation. Have you ever felt that you have been treated badly by someone either on the phone or in a store? – you are probably reluctant to return to that company. So regardless of the amount of money invested in the marketing mix, that company lost your business because one member of staff was impolite.

The media is a strong influence in the UK markets. Approximately five million people read the *Sun* every day. The media has the power to influence customer opinion. Recently, Marks and Spencer has suffered from bad publicity because of its dealings with suppliers. This media coverage may have resulted in the loss of valuable customers for the retailer. Chapter 11 discusses publicity management in some detail. It can be a powerful tool in marketing if it is managed well. However, you must remember that, as with other micro environmental factors, organisations can attempt to influence the media but they do not have direct control over the stories that newspapers print.

The public at large, the local community and pressure groups also have an impact on organisational strategy. When BMW decided to sell Rover, the ensuing threat to the future of the UK manufacturer generated a degree of ill-feeling in the UK towards the German company.

IT and the External Environment

Monitoring the external environment is an onerous task for any organisation. It requires constant information gathering and monitoring of many variable factors.

Nowadays, sophisticated computer programmes aid the marketer's task. Programmes can monitor economic factors to identify and forecast trends. This will help the marketer to forecast future sales for products.

The internet also provides a relatively quick means of gathering information about environmental trends and stakeholder activities. You can access information on economic trends, social trends and, for more specific research, you might access competitors' web sites.

Summary

This chapter has overviewed the elements of the macro and micro environment. Both environments are uncontrollable but have a direct influence on marketing strategy. Because of this, information must be gathered during the audit stage of the marketing planning process. However, even when not doing an audit, it is advisable for organisations to constantly monitor these ever-changing environments.

The macro environment contains the PEST factors. The micro environment is formed of customers, suppliers, competitors, intermediaries and publics. Although uncontrollable, the organisation can have some influence over the members of the micro environment.

Review Questions

1. What are the environments that an organisation operates in?
2. Why must these environments be monitored?
3. Why are the members of these environments uncontrollable?
4. List five political factors that impact on an organisation.
5. List five social trends in Britain.

6. What are Porter's Five Forces?

7. Explain the conditions that exist when bargaining power of suppliers is strong.

8. Why is it important to build relationships with suppliers?

9. Explain the impact of the media on an organisation.

10. What is business-to-business marketing?

Discussion Questions

1. Explain how political/legal factors impact on marketing strategy.

2. Select an industry with which you are familiar. Carry out a competitive analysis of this industry.

3. Explain how technology has impacted on an industry of your choice.

4. Identify the likely competitors of:

    -BT

    -National Express Coaches

    -BHS.

5. Using examples, discuss the impact of social trends on marketing strategy.

Key Terms

Business-to-business marketing	Economic factors	Porter
Buyers' power	Intermediaries	Publics
Competitive rivalry	Internal marketing	Relationship marketing
Competitors	Macro environment	Social factors
Customers	Me-too products	Substitutes
Demographics	Micro environment	Supplier's power
Derived demand	PEST factors	Suppliers
	Political factors	Technological factors

Chapter 4

Marketing Research

Introduction

Chapter 3 highlighted the importance of gathering information about customers and other macro and micro environmental factors. To be able to satisfy customers, organisations must understand their needs and wants. The way to gather such information is through marketing research.

Marketing research includes gathering information on the factors listed in Figure 4.1. This list is by no means exhaustive but it gives you an indication of the scope of marketing research. Organisations are unlikely to gather information on all of these factors at any one time and they may have individual research projects taking place at varying times. Research is essential because the macro and micro environment is constantly changing and so organisations must respond to these changes. Marketing research should help an organisation to reduce the need to react to environmental changes by helping the organisation to be more ready for change.

Many organisations enlist the help of a research agency because effective marketing research is difficult. Many issues arise that are often unforeseen. The quality of information gathered may depend on the people involved in the process. An agency offers some expertise in this area.

Research Areas	FACTORS THAT MAY BE CONSIDERED
Customer research	Influences on buying behaviour
	Impact of selling activities
	Customer attitudes to company/products
	Causes of complaints
	Size of market
	Market trends
	Potential market size
	Sales forecasting
Product research	Design, development, testing of new products
	Improvement of existing products
	Forecasting likely trends in customer preferences
	Packaging design
Sales research	Examination of current selling activities
	Sales by territory
	Sales force effectiveness
	Cost of sales
	Sales forecasting
Pricing research	Analysis of demand elasticity
	Analysis of costs
	Customer perceptions of price
	Price sensitivities
Promotion research	Evaluation of effectiveness cf advertising
	Evaluation of effectiveness of public relations
	Evaluation of effectiveness of sales promotions
Distribution research	Location of distribution centres
	Packaging for transportation
	Intermediary requirements
	Costs of methods of transportation

Figure 4.1 The Scope of Marketing Research

The Research Process

Research is a costly activity and so should be planned. Figure 4.2 illustrates the stages that should be followed when carrying out marketing research. By following this process, the organisation will be more assured of gathering reliable and valid information that addresses the key research objectives.

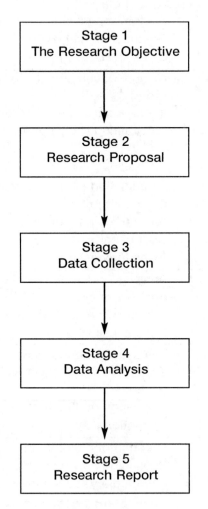

Figure 4.2 The Marketing Research Process
Adapted from Chisnall, Marketing Research

Stage 1: The Research Objective

This stage of the process is critical to the success of the research that will be performed. The research brief actually defines the marketing problem or objective that the entire research will be focused on. Without a clear objective, research will be costly and may result in useless information and results. The research objective is likely to be concerned with some of the areas indicated in Figure 4.1.

Stage 2: Research Proposal

This is perhaps the most complex part of the research process. Once the objective has been defined, the proposal defines how the information will be gathered.   The remaining stages of the process should be straightforward if the research proposal is detailed and thorough. The following information is required within the research proposal:

◆ secondary data sources

◆ the population to be surveyed

◆ the sample method and size

◆ primary data collection methods

◆ timing/scheduling

◆ staff requirements

◆ costs.

This chapter will look at population, sampling and methodology is some detail as many decisions must be taken within this stage of the research.

Stage 3: Data Collection

This stage simply involves putting the research proposal into practice. If the proposal has been clearly defined, then data collection simply involves following the plan. However, this is the costliest stage of the research and so efficiency is important.

Stage 4: Data Analysis

Once the research has been carried out, the data gathered can be studied and analysed to extract meaning. Analysis can be complex but there are numerous computer packages available on the market to better manage both quantitive and qualitative data (see page 46).

Stage 5: The Research Report

The findings from the data analysis are usually presented in report format. The report usually contains some interpretation of the data analysis. It is at this stage that the research objective is fully addressed.

Secondary Data

Secondary research is usually performed before any primary research is undertaken. Secondary data comes from research which has been carried out by someone else. Primary data is generated by an organisation to directly address the research objectives – it involves physically performing the research.

Because secondary data is not generated by the organisation itself, it is cheaper and much quicker to gather. Such data can come from newspapers, books, the web, research agencies, television and government reports. Secondary research is also known as desk research. There are two sources of secondary data:

Internal sources: organisations generate a massive amount of information. This information is valuable for research purposes. Sales figures, cost analysis, stock records, customer complaints and staff reports often provide valuable information.

External sources: apart from those already mentioned, there are multitude of external secondary sources of information. These include Kompas, the Annual Abstract of Statistics, Monthly Digest of Statistics, UK Balance of Payments, Anbar management publications, business periodicals, Kelly's Manufacturing and Merchants yearbook, trade associations. The sources of external secondary information are endless.

Any good library has a variety of sources of information (much of which can also be accessed via the internet).

Apart from the fact that secondary data is relatively easy and inexpensive to gather, it offers various other advantages:

Secondary data may actually directly address the research objective. This means there may be no need to perform primary research.

It may help to redefine the research objective or indicate areas that should be tested during primary research.

It can be used as an aid in designing the primary research techniques. Secondary research may show how previous researchers have tackled similar problems.

It may help to define the population that should be researched (see section on Population and Sampling).

However, secondary research also has some drawbacks:

Previous research was not designed to directly address the current research objectives. Therefore, interpretation is often necessary.

Although cheaper than primary research, some secondary research reports can costs several thousand pounds to purchase.

Secondary sources may already be out-of-date considering the nature of the macro environment.

Secondary data that actually suits the researchers needs may not be available.

The secondary data may not be reliable. The researcher should understand how the data was collected and by whom before basing any decisions on it. The internet is often criticised as a basis of secondary research because the validity of the data gathered on it cannot always be established.

Population and Sampling

Once secondary research has been performed, the organisation is ready to plan primary research. This begins with a definition of the population to be researched. In research terms, the population is not simply the whole of the UK. Instead, it is the population that the research objectives are directly concerned with.

For instance, a clothing manufacturer wishing to assess the response to a new line of ladies clothes might define the population for research as women. If the manufacturer sold premium priced clothing to women in the 25-30 year-old age bracket and wanted to assess the response to a new line of clothing then the research population would be women between the ages of 25-30 years of age who earn over £25,000 per annum.

It is important to define the population characteristics so that a sample can be selected. A sample is a group of people from the population who will actually take part in the primary research. It would not be feasible to question all women in a population with the characteristics mentioned and so a proportion or sample of that population is selected. The results drawn from the sample are representative of the research population as a whole.

Because the results drawn from the sample will be representative of the entire research population, selection of the sample is important. There are various methods to select samples. Generally, there are two main types of sampling: probability and non-probability sampling.

Probability Sampling Techniques

Simple random sampling: this means that every member of the identified population has an equal chance of being involved in the research. The use of random tables or 'pulling names from hats' can be used to generate the sample. Software packages are now available that will select a random sample once all of the elements of the population are entered.

Stratified sampling: this method involves further subdivision of the population to be surveyed. Going back to the population we discussed earlier (women, 25-30 year old, +£25,000 income) the researcher may realise that women live in different geographical regions within the UK. To ensure that each region is represented in the sample, the research will stratify the population into sub groups and select a random sample from each of these groups. The sample drawn should be representative of the whole population. So, if 35% of the entire population come from the South East of England, then 35% of the sample selected should be from the South East of England.

Cluster sampling: once again, the population is divided into sub groups except in this case they are called clusters. In this case, a random selection of clusters is then made. So, if the clusters are geographical regions (see above), then a random sample of the clusters might result with Greater Manchester, the Midlands and Greater London. A further random sample is then selected from inside each of the sampled clusters.

Multi-stage sampling: as already described, clusters are drawn from a population. Multi-stage sampling recognises that these clusters may be different in size. A cluster that is twice the size of the other clusters will have twice the chance of selection. Further clusters are then identified.

Non-probability sampling

Convenience sampling: this sampling method is quick and relatively low in cost. In the case of the clothes manufacturer we have been discussing, a convenience sample might involve the researcher asking any women that work in the factory for their opinions of the new clothing range. It is a quick method but results should be treated with some caution.

Judgement sampling: here, some attempt is made to ensure that the sample is representative of the population. The research might only question women in the local vicinity that appear to fit the population characteristics.

Purposive sampling: this sampling method does not make any attempt at being representative of the population. Instead, the sample is formed of members that meet conditions that are appropriate to the investigation. For instance, the ladies' clothes manufacturer might question 100 designers in Britain to ask for their opinion of the new clothing range.

Quota sampling: this method involves selecting members of a sample in the same proportion as they occur in the total population. The population is stratified by sex, age, income (as discussed above). Quotas are then provided to interviewers who are given the responsibility of questioning respondents that meet the quota. For instance, a researcher might be given a quota of 25 women in total. Twenty of the women must earn between £25,000 and £35,000 and five women should earn over £35,000. It is up to the interviewer to ensure the quota is fulfilled.

Primary Research

Primary research, sometimes known as field research, involves gathering data that directly addresses the research objectives. It is a costly and time consuming activity and should be planned carefully.

Before deciding on the primary research technique, it is necessary for the researcher to decide the type of information required to address the research objectives. There are two approaches to generating information.

Qualitative research: This type of research seeks to find out what may account for certain kinds of behaviour. It generally asks the questions 'how', 'why' and 'what'. It looks for attitudes, opinions, reasons and feelings.

Quantitative research: This type of research addresses the 'how many' question. For instance, how many people will buy a product at x price or how many people prefer red rather than blue packaging.

The type of information required will aid the researcher in deciding the appropriate primary research technique. There are three methods of generating primary information: observation, experimentation and surveys.

Observation: observing people and their activities for a purpose and to address research objectives provides a valuable source of information about behaviour. Almost every time you go into a shop you are being observed on camera. This may be for security purposes primarily but it is also used as a research tool.

Through observation, researchers can watch the route you take through a store, the items you touch and feel and the selections you make. All of this is valuable information, especially in light of the fact that you are unaware that you are being observed and so will behave naturally.

Rival companies also use observation to check prices and display techniques in retail stores.

Although observation reveals valuable information about behaviour, it does not reveal feelings or motives. It is quite limited in scope.

Experimentation: this method of primary research involves setting up an experiment where certain variables are tested. Usually, experimentation is used to test elements of the marketing mix. For instance, the researcher might change the colour of packaging to see if sales are affected or perhaps the price is changed to see if sales increase. Usually, one variable is tested at a time.

A good example of experimentation is 'blind' taste testing. The consumer is asked to taste various products and rate them for, say, taste and texture. The researcher is then able to identify the best-tasting product without the influence of advertising and brand names.

Surveys: the most common form of primary research is the use of questionnaires. You have probably completed several questionnaires asking for your opinion about products and services. Questionnaires are difficult to design and it is advisable to use the skills of an expert in questionnaire design. They are often formed of both open and closed questions. Open questions generate qualitative information while closed questions usually generate quantitative information.

There are three common methods for issuing questionnaires: by mail, by telephone and by personal interviewing.

Mail: questionnaires are posted to the sample group who then complete and return it.

Advantages:

◆ It is a relatively inexpensive method of doing primary research.

◆ It allows a large sample to be researched.

◆ It eliminates the problem of interviewer bias.

◆ It is useful for quantitative information.

◆ Respondents can complete the questionnaire when it is convenient to them.

Disadvantages:

◆ It does not generate a high response rate. Respondents may not complete the questionnaire and return it.

◆ The researcher can never be sure who has actually completed the questionnaire.

◆ Questions must be simple and concise to ensure respondent understands them.

◆ Only a limited amount of open questions can be used.

Telephone: researchers telephone respondents and ask questions.

Advantages:

◆ It allows the researcher to enter responses directly onto computer systems for analysis and is therefore relatively quick.

◆ It allows the respondent to take part in the survey at a convenient time.

◆ The interviewer can ask for clarification of answers or explain difficult questions.

◆ It usually achieves a higher response rate that mail questionnaires.

Disadvantages:

◆ Respondents are often wary of telephone research because they fear it may a be sales call.

◆ Respondents can simply put the phone down.

◆ Researchers cannot use pictures or symbols to aid their research.

◆ The sample is limited to respondents who can be contacted by telephone.

Personal interviewing: trained interviewers ask questions to a selected sample of people either at home, work or in the street.

Advantages:

♦ The interviewer can explain questions and probe for responses.

♦ The interviewer can check with the respondent that they are part of the sample to be questioned (see quota sampling).

♦ The interviewer can ensure all relevant questions are answered.

♦ It is good for qualitative information.

♦ The researcher can gather additional information through observation of the respondent.

♦ Props and pictures can be used during the interview.

Disadvantages:

♦ The interviewers must be well trained and motivated so that they do not cause bias (leading respondents and influencing their answers).

♦ It is time consuming and costly.

♦ It requires a lot of planning.

♦ It is suitable only for smaller sample sizes.

Panel research: respondents take part in a survey over a period of time. Unlike the other methods of research, respondents answer the same questions at periodic intervals - perhaps every three months.

Advantages:

♦ The researcher can gather information on trends.

♦ The sample only has to be selected once.

♦ Respondents become familiar with the research and are more likely to provide accurate responses.

♦ It often achieves a high response rate.

Disadvantages:

♦ Panel members may drop out.

◆ Respondents may become self-conscious and adjust their own behaviour rather than acting naturally.

Group discussions: groups of 8-12 respondents are brought together to discuss issues raised by the researcher.

Advantages:

◆ It is good for qualitative information.

◆ It is quicker and cheaper than personal interviews.

◆ Researchers can gather additional information through observation of the group.

◆ Group members stimulate each other which generates more discussion.

Disadvantages:

◆ There is usually a small sample size.

◆ Quieter respondents may not participate.

◆ It is very difficult to analyse the data generated.

◆ It requires careful planning and co-ordination.

IT and Marketing Research

The internet offers obvious advantages for secondary research. The researcher has almost unlimited access to a wide range of information. However, a word of caution is necessary here. Web sites can be established by anyone. When using the internet as a research tool, the researcher should check the source of the information being provided.

The internet is also useful for performing primary research. The researcher can put a questionnaire onto a web site and encourage visitors to that web site to complete it. This is not a completely scientific means of sampling. However, useful information can be generated. It is perhaps more suited to primary research when convenience sampling is being used.

There are also many computer programmes available to the researcher to aid the analysis of large amounts of quantitative data.

Summary

Marketing research is a costly and time consuming activity and therefore requires careful planning and co-ordination. It is often advisable to use the skills and expertise of a market research agency to ensure that the information generated is useful. Although research is expensive, organisations need to understand their customers in order to remain ahead of competitors. The organisation that best satisfies customers will remain profitable and generate customer loyalty.

The research process provides the basis for a logical approach to performing the research. After defining the research objectives, the researcher can plan both secondary and primary research techniques.

Review Questions

1. What type of information can be gathered using marketing research?
2. What are the five stages of the research process?
3. What is qualitative information?
4. Why should secondary research always be carried out before primary research?
5. What is sampling?
6. Explain three methods of probability sampling.
7. List three advantages of mail surveys.
8. Why should marketing research be performed?

Discussion Questions

1. Identify and justify the research technique you would recommend for an organisation wishing to decide on the colour of packaging for its products.

2. Write a marketing research plan for an organisation wishing to discover consumer attitudes to a new product.

3. How would you sample students from your company/college if you were conducting a survey into the canteen?

Key Terms

Bias	Panel research	Questionnaire
Experimentation	Personal interviewing	Sampling
Group discussion	Population	Secondary data
Mail survey	Primary data	Survey
Marketing research	Probability sampling	Telephone survey
Non-probability sampling	Qualitative research	
Observation	Quantitative research	

Chapter 5
Consumer Buying Behaviour

Introduction

Customer satisfaction is the key to organisational success. Therefore, understanding customers is crucial. Customers buy goods and services for different reasons and often display complex buying behaviour. The research techniques described in Chapter 4 help the marketer to gain a better understanding of buying behaviour. It is only through understanding buying behaviour that the marketer can attempt to satisfy customers. In this chapter we will look at consumer buying behaviour. In Chapter 6 we will look at organisational buying behaviour.

Consumers are defined as 'purchasers of goods and services for immediate use and consumption' (*The International Dictionary of Management*). Consumers buy goods for themselves or for their households to satisfy their own needs and wants.

Organisations or organisational buyers purchase goods and services for their organisations to satisfy the needs of the organisation. Both consumers and organisations are customers.

The Consumer Buying Process

Consumers make purchases to satisfy their own needs. Often, they follow a series of steps so that they select the right product or service that will satisfy these needs. Figure 5.1 displays the decision making process that a consumer will follow when making a buying decision.

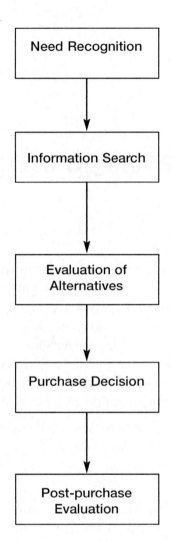

Figure 5.1 Consumer Decision Making Process

Need Recognition

Before a purchase is initiated, the consumer becomes aware of a need. This need could be internally driven such as hunger or thirst or externally driven such as an advertisement for a new item of clothing that stimulates the need. In either case, the consumer is driven to satisfy the need.

Information Search

Once the consumer recognises the need, s/he will be driven to satisfying that need. If the need is usual, such as hunger, the consumer may rely on past experience of what satisfies this need. For instance, if you are hungry, you might buy a Big Mac because you know, from past experience, that this food satisfies your internally driven need.

However, if the need is unusual or unfamiliar the consumer may seek additional information. In this case, the consumer may seek information from family, friends, the media, sales people or by actually testing or trialing the product. Buying a new car is a much bigger decision than selecting the type of food that will best satisfy your hunger. If you were considering purchasing a car you might start to pay attention to car magazines and car advertisements. You might ask friends or family about their experiences with cars and you might visit a showroom to get information from the sales people there. It is only through this information search that you can identify the means of satisfying your need.

Evaluation of Alternatives

Once the information search is complete, the consumer will evaluate the alternatives. Using our example of buying a new car, the consumer may consider price and engine size to be key to their purchase decision. The consumer will evaluate the information gathered to select the car that best meets the price and engine requirements.

Purchase Decision

The consumer makes the purchase. It is important to remember that, until the customer actually buys the product, s/he can withdraw from the buying process.

Post Purchase Evaluation

Once the consumer has purchased the product or service, s/he will evaluate and assess whether the product has met the needs identified at the first stage of the decision making process. This is known as post purchase evaluation. This is an important stage and cannot be ignored by marketers. Remember, marketing is about customer satisfaction. A satisfied customer may purchase the product again in the future and may recommend the product to friends and family (when they are in the information search stage).

Cognitive dissonance can occur at this stage of the decision making process. Cognitive dissonance refers to the doubts consumers have after making a purchase. If the consumer is unhappy or dissatisfied, the organisation may suffer from damaging word of mouth and the consumer may not buy from the organisation again.

Throughout this process the marketer can influence the consumer. At the need recognition stage, the marketer can use promotion to stimulate consumer needs. At the information search stage, the marketer can provide sales literature, advertisements, media articles, informative and persuasive packaging to provide information to the consumer.

During the evaluation of alternatives stage it is important that the marketer understands how consumers evaluate products. By understanding the evaluative process the marketer can take steps to influence it. In the case of cars, advertisements may be changed to provide more detail on price or engine size, for example, or sales people may be trained to talk about price and negotiate with the consumer.

At the purchase decision stage it is important that the marketer does not assume that the consumer will actually buy the product. The consumer can drop out of the decision making stage at any time. It is important that the consumer receives high levels of service and that information generated during the search stage is confirmed at this stage. Otherwise, the consumer may seek to satisfy his need by purchasing a competitor's product.

The marketer may take steps to reduce cognitive dissonance during the post purchase evaluation stage. Many organisations offer consumers the opportunity to return their goods. The marketer can seek consumer views about their purchases and provide supportive information about their purchases. For instance, the consumer that continually sees advertisements about the car s/he has just purchased may be reassured that s/he made the right decision.

Influences on Decision Making

Throughout the decision making process, consumers are influenced by many variables. Figure 5.2 indicates the influences that affect consumers. It is important for the marketer to understand these influences as they may affect any stage of the decision making process and may result in the consumer deciding not to purchase. The marketer is unlikely to be able to control these influences so they could be detrimental to customer satisfaction.

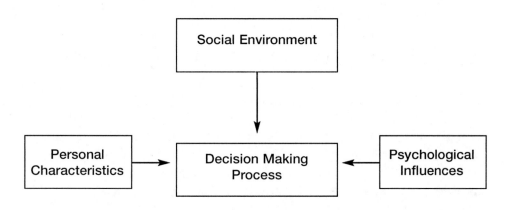

Figure 5.2 Influences on the Consumer Decision Making Process

Social Environment

According to Hill and O'Sullivan, the social environment consists of culture, reference groups and social class.

Culture: consumers learn and acquire a culture. It is the beliefs and norms of any society and it is fundamental to individual needs and wants. Societies and countries vary in their culture. For instance, there is a tradition of siestas (afternoon rests) in certain Mediterranean countries. Other cultural differences might be the emphasis placed by a society on the importance of owning a car, or of owning one's own home rather than renting. Different food types are also often associated with different cultures. Each of these areas of our lives stimulate needs which we will attempt to satisfy.

Reference groups: consumer behaviour is also influenced by various groups within society. These groups are known as reference groups and are often used during the information search of the decision making process. They include, among others:

- family
- friends
- colleagues
- religious groups
- professional associates
- trade unions.

Social class: a social class is a set of people with similar social and economic circumstances. You've probably used the terms working class, middle class and upper class. It is more accepted to refer to class in terms of socio-economic groups (see Figure 5.3). Consumers tend to have a lot of interaction with individuals in the same socio-economic grouping as themselves. Consumers in the socio-economic grouping tend to exhibit the same type of buying behaviour. Think about newspapers. It is more likely for consumers from socio-economic groupings A and B to buy the *Financial Times*. It is more likely for consumers from C2, D and E to buy the *Sun*. Such judgements involve assumptions but it is important to the marketer to be able to group people with similar buying behaviour. This issue is explored in some depth in Chapter 7.

Grade	Description	Examples
A	Higher managerial, administrative or professional	Accountants, solicitors, company directors.
B	Middle to senior management	Department heads
C1	Junior management, supervisory and clerical workers	Secretaries, clerks
C2	Skilled manual workers	Plumbers, carpenters, electricians
D	Semi-skilled or unskilled workers	Production line staff
E	Pensioners, casual workers, widows	

Figure 5.3 Socio-economic Groupings

Personal Characteristics

According to Kotler, personal characteristics include age, life-cycle stage, occupation, economic situation, life style and personality.

Age and life-cycle stage: age and life stage have a major influence on consumer buying decisions. If you think about cars, a younger consumer may want a car to display an image to reference groups. A more mature consumer with children may purchase a car that is roomy, economical to run and safe to drive. Figure 5.4 displays the life cycle stages that many consumers pass through. At each stage of the life-cycle, consumers are likely to have different needs and wants. You may notice that, although many consumers pass through these life-cycle stages, our culture is continually evolving and there are exceptions to this process.

STAGE	DESCRIPTION
Bachelor stage	Young single people not living at home
Newly married couples	Young, no children
Full nest 1	Youngest child under six
Full nest 2	Youngest child over six
Full nest 3	Older married couples, with dependent children
Empty nest 1	Older married couples, without dependent children
Empty nest 2	Older married couples, no dependent children, head retired
Solitary survivor	In labour force
Solitary survivor	Retired

Figure 5.4   Stages of the Life-Cycle

Occupation: Figure 5.3 detailed socio-economic groupings and the types of jobs usual for each group.   An individual's job affects the products s/he buys.   For instance, an A might buy suits and expensive travel while a C2 might purchase more casual clothes and package holidays.   It is perhaps slightly offensive to make such assumptions, but marketers are attempting to satisfy millions of consumers every day.   So, some generalisation has to be made.   Think about your friends.   Are they in similar jobs to you?   Do you wear similar types of clothing?   Are you all of similar ages?

Economic situation: although income is often linked to socio-economic groupings, this is not always necessarily the case.   During recessions, consumer income may decrease (see Chapter 3).   This means that marketers may have to think about pricing their products differently.

Life style: this is the way we live. It is about our hobbies, interests and opinions. These may be closely related to our life-cycle stage as well as our socio-economic grouping. Our life style strongly influences the way we spend our money. Marketers, again, attempt to group people that have similar life styles.

Personality: your own personality will influence your buying behaviour. You may be shy or aggressive, self-assured or insecure, dominant or dominated. Marketers will attempt to understand personalities so that products and services better satisfy consumers. Club 18-30 seems to target consumers that are looking for fun.

Psychological Influences

Motivation and perception also influence consumer buying decisions. *The International Dictionary of Management* defines motivation as 'processes or factors that cause people to act or behave in certain ways'. These processes or factors are needs that cause people to act in certain ways to satisfy them. One of the most recognised motivational theories is Maslow's Hierarchy of Needs (see Figure 5.5). The hierarchy explains that, first, individuals want to satisfy physiological needs (food, warmth, etc). Once these needs are satisfied, individuals will seek to satisfy safety needs (security, protection, etc). As each level of needs is satisfied, individuals move to the next need level.

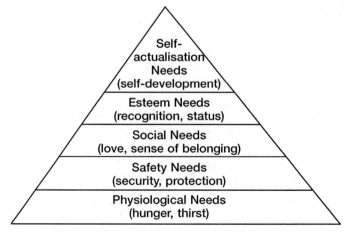

Figure 5.5 Maslow's Hierarchy of Needs

For marketers, Maslow's Hierarchy is a valuable tool for analysing consumer needs. As consumers become more affluent, they may seek to satisfy higher level needs. This is one of the reasons that brands are so successful. Famous names like Gucci, Prada and Calvin Klein often satisfy more than the basic needs. They offer individuals the chance satisfy needs such as self-esteem and status.

The issue of motivation is further influenced by perception. Two people with the same needs or motivation may act very differently because they perceive the situation differently. For instance, if two individuals see an advertisement, one may find it interesting and appealing, another might find it false, misleading or even offensive. Individuals tend to have selective retention so that they only remember those things that are important to them as individuals. So the marketer has to deal with all the influences we have discussed as well as different perceptions of a situation. The consumer displays complex buying behaviour. It is only through research that the marketer can understand this behaviour and attempt to satisfy consumer needs.

Participants in the Buying Process

Alongside the decision making process and the influences on consumer decisions, there are various participants in the buying process. These are the people, or organisations, that are actually involved when the consumer makes a purchase. There are five consumer buying participants or roles:

Suggester: the person who comes up with the idea to buy something.

Purchaser: the person who actually pays for the goods.

Advisor: the person or organisation that advises on the purchase. This could be a company sales person or an advertisement.

Decider: the person that actually makes the decision on what to buy, when to buy and how to buy.

End-user: the person who actually uses or consumes the product.

This consumer decision making unit is easily remembered by the acronym SPADE. It may involve only one individual or several individuals and organisations.

If you were purchasing a product to satisfy your hunger, then you might take on all of these roles. For less familiar products, several different participants will be involved. Using our example of purchasing a car the following participants may be involved:

Suggester: a friend suggests that you may save money in the long term if you bought a more reliable car.

Purchaser: you pay for the car.

Advisor: you rely on sales literature and the salesperson to tell you about the car and also take advice from your friends.

Decider: you make the decision to purchase on an interest free arrangement.

End-user: both you and your friend.

You can see from this example that more people are involved in the decision making unit.

Summary

Consumer buying behaviour is complex but it is only through an understanding of this behaviour that the marketer can satisfy needs and encourage customer loyalty. It is through effective marketing research that information on buyer behaviour can be gathered.

Consumers usually follow a logical buying process when making purchases and the marketer can attempt to influence the consumer at each stage of the buying process. However, this process is made more complex by the additional influences on it. These influences include personal characteristics, psychological influences and the social environment. There is also the added complexity that while actually making the purchase there are various participants within the decision making unit.

Review Questions

1. What is the difference between a consumer and a customer?

2. What are the stages involved in the consumer buying process?

3. List the three major types of influence on the consumer buying process.

4. What are the socio-economic groups that exist?

5. Explain the concept of motivation.

6. How does age affect buying behaviour?

7. Explain the concept of lifestyle and its influence on consumer buying behaviour.

8. What are the roles in the consumer decision making unit?

Discussion Questions

1. Describe three advertisements with which you are familiar. What type of people do you think these advertisements are attempting to influence?

2. Identify examples of advertisements that appeal to each of the motivations identified in Maslow's Hierarchy of Needs.

3. Who may be involved in the decision making unit for:

    -a new television?

    -a pair of designer jeans?

    -a toothpaste?

    -the annual family holiday?

4. If you were involved in the design of packaging for a new type of chocolate bar, what type of consumer information would you need?

Key Terms

Buying behaviour	Decision making unit	Psychological influences
Cognitive dissonance	Lifecycle	Reference groups
Consumer	Lifestyle	Social class
Culture	Motivation	Social environment
Customer	Perception	Socio-economic grouping
	Personality	SPADE

Chapter 6
Organisational Buying Behaviour

Introduction

Organisational buying behaviour is complex and must be understood by the marketer if organisational needs are to be satisfied. Organisational buyers are purchasing products and services to satisfy the needs of the organisation. In other words, one organisation is buying from another organisation. This activity is commonly known as business-to-business marketing. There are three types of organisational buying.

Industrial buying: this involves organisations acquiring goods and services that are used in the production of other goods and services. For example, Heinz may buy aluminium to produce cans for their products.

Resale buying: this involves organisations acquiring goods and services to resell. For example, Tesco buys Heinz baked beans to sell to the consumer market.

Institutional buying: this is usually associated with government departments and institutions that buy goods to carry out their main functions. For example, the NHS buys medical supplies so that it can service its patients.

As with consumer purchasing, the marketer is still concerned with meeting organisational needs. These needs are often consumer driven (see derived demand, Chapter 3) and so the buying behaviour displayed by organisations is often complex. Added to this is the fact that many organisations have professional buying teams which the marketer must deal with effectively.

The Organisational Buying Process

Because organisational buying decisions are often of strategic importance, the buying process is usually more lengthy than in consumer markets. The purchase may involve large sums of money and may be technically complex. In the case of large purchases there may be many people actually involved in the buying process. Figure 6.1 displays the organisational buying process. You can see from this diagram that it is a longer and more complex process than that involved in consumer buying.

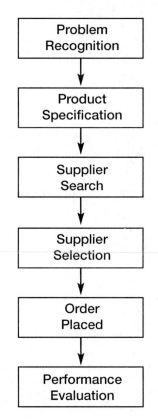

Figure 6.1 The Organisational Buying Process
(Adapted from Lancaster and Reynolds, Marketing)

Problem Recognition

Organisational buying usually starts with someone in the organisation identifying a need. This might be the purchaser or another user in the organisation. For instance, on a production line, it might be the supervisor that realises one machine is constantly breaking down and wasting resources. The supervisor might then initiate the buying process by informing the purchasing department of the problem. The marketing department within the buying organisation could be developing a new product and so the purchasing department may get involved in buying the materials necessary to make the new product.

Unlike consumer buying, organisational buying is usually planned. There are not so many incidences of impulse purchasing.

Product Specification

The organisational purchaser will usually draw up a specification of the product to be purchased. This specification might include such details as the quality, quantity and price of the item to be purchased. It is unusual for the purchaser to draw up the specification in isolation. The specification is developed in conjunction with other departments in the organisation.

Supplier Search

The purchaser will identify potential suppliers of the products. This information might come from previous experience, from recommendations or from advertisements in trade directories and magazines. The purchaser may ask prospective suppliers to submit proposals or to give presentations about their products. It is imperative at this stage that as much information as possible is gathered. The product specification should be met and it is only through research that the buyer can ensure this is the case.

At this stage, marketers from the supplying organisation should also be doing research. They need to fully understand the company and the product specification of the buying organisation. This is imperative as they will be competing for the business.

Supplier Selection

The supplier that best meets the product specification is most likely to be selected. However, this is often not as straightforward as it appears. Several suppliers may be able to provide the products necessary and so the purchaser must make a selection. It is common to rank the desired attributes of potential suppliers to aid the supplier selection decision. Apart from meeting the product specification, the purchaser might look at after-sales service, delivery schedules and communication channels. The purchaser will select the supplier that offers the best overall deal.

Marketers in the supplying organisation should understand their competitors and the purchasers to ensure they are meeting the needs of the purchasing organisation.

Order Placed

Once a selection is made, the purchaser can place the order. The supplier should remember that, until the order is placed, the purchaser can still drop out of the process.

Actually placing the order may be complex. Both the buyer and the seller may be involved in lengthy negotiations and contract discussions. It is important that both parties understand their full obligations to fulfil the needs of the buying organisation.

Marketers in the supplying organisation often have to develop effective negotiation skills to manage this stage of the process effectively.

Performance Evaluation

After the purchase is made, the purchaser will evaluate whether the product has met the organisational needs. As in consumer buying, this stage is the key to satisfaction. If the purchaser is satisfied, s/he may use the supplier again and recommend the supplier to colleagues. Dissatisfaction can result in long-term loss of business.

This process is more thorough than that of consumer buying behaviour and because of its complexity and the number of people involved, the business-to-business marketer must thoroughly understand its customers. Business markets have several characteristics that differentiate them from consumer markets:

◆ purchases may be higher in value
◆ purchases may occur much less frequently
◆ there are fewer organisations (potential buyers) than consumers.

These characteristics mean that the loss of one sale may impact on the business marketer much more than in consumer marketing. Markets are now more concerned with building relationships in business-to-business markets rather than in achieving one-off sales.

If the relationship (often called a partnership by purchasers) is established, the marketer can secure more long-term business. The relationship may encourage the purchasing organisation not to seek information from other suppliers throughout the buying process. The relationship may result in lower costs for both the supplier and the buyer because both parties understand each others needs better.

It is also important for the marketer to understand the importance of the buying decision. If the decision is key to achieving strategic goals, the buying decision may be a lengthy one. However, some decisions, such as stationery buying, are much more straightforward. In this case, once the supplier has been selected, the buying organisation may not go through the entire process every time more stationery is ordered. For ease, buying decisions can be classified under three main headings.

Straight rebuying: products that require little purchasing effort because they are routine purchases. Straightforward re-ordering is often used by the buying organisation. Examples may include pens, headed paper, business cards.

Modified rebuying: this occurs when there is a change in the buying organisation's needs. Changes in product specifications may mean the search for a new supplier. This type of buying may originate from straight rebuying situations.

New task: this involves buying unfamiliar or expensive products such as new computer systems or new machinery. Because of the risk involved the buying process may be lengthy and involve many people.

Influences on Decision Making

Business buying is a professional process but there are many influences on the organisational purchaser. It would be wrong to assume that the main influence on the decision is price. Figure 6.2 indicates the influences on the organisational purchaser. The market needs to understand these influences in order to satisfy the needs of the organisation and its purchasers.

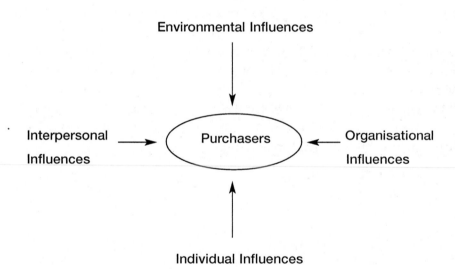

Figure 6.2 Organisational Buying Influences
(Adapted from Kotler & Armstrong, Principles of Marketing)

Environmental Factors

Because the buying decision is often strategic, purchasers may be influenced by the state of the economy and economic forecasts. If the products being purchased are in short supply then the purchaser may wish to build a better relationship with the supplying organisation. If the economy is growing and higher levels of demand are forecast, the purchaser may again wish to secure regular sources of supply.

Organisational Factors

Most organisations have objectives, structures, procedures and processes that are specific to them. All of these factors impact on the buying decision. The marketer should understand organisation factors because they directly affect how the buying decision is made and who is involved in the decision. For instance, the purchaser may be the main point of contact for the marketer, but the accountant or managing director may have the power to make the decision.

In some organisations, the purchasing department is centralised meaning that purchasing decisions for the entire organisation are made centrally in one office. This may be beneficial for the marketer who deals with only one department. In other organisations, where there are many branches, for instance retailers, buying decisions may be decentralised. This means that each subsidiary or branch has its own purchasing department. Each of these purchasing departments may behave quite differently and so the marketer has the added complexity of understanding different buying departments within the one organisation.

Interpersonal Factors

Because of the strategic importance of organisational purchasing, there are often many participants in the decision making unit. Figure 6.3 displays the roles in the organisational decision making unit. Each of these participants has a direct influence throughout the buying process.

ROLE	DESCRIPTION
Gatekeepers	People who control the flow of information to others. It may be a receptionist that does not pass sales literature to the buying department.
Users	People who actually use the products and who may initiate the buying process and help with developing product specifications.
Influencers	People who influence the buying decision. They help to develop the product specification and may provide information about suppliers.
Buyers	People who have the authority to select the supplier and pay for the products. This is not always the purchaser, it may be an accountant.
Deciders	People who select the supplier.

Figure 6.3 The Organisational Decision Making Unit
(Adapted from Chisnall, Strategic Business Marketing)

Alongside the professional roles identified in Figure 6.3, buying participants have a personal influence on the buying decision. Each participant may have his own motivations and priorities. The gatekeeper may have a poor relationship with the decider and so may not pass on information from the supplier. The buyer may be motivated by status and power and so may disagree with the decider's decisions because of this.

Marketers in the supplying organisation must deal with these professional buying roles as well as the interpersonal factors that exist. The interpersonal factors are often not obvious but the marketer must be aware of them.

Individual Factors

We have already mentioned that individuals bring in their own personal motivations to the buying process. These personal or individual factors are influenced by age, income, education, personality, etc. To fully understand the buying process, the marketer needs to understand the participants in the decision making unit and their own personal motivations.

Summary

Marketers should attempt to satisfy organisational needs to ensure long-term relationships. However, organisational buying behaviour is complex and is affected by many factors.

There are six key stages in the organisational buying process and there are many participants in the buying decision. These participants are influenced by business factors such as the economic situation and organisational objectives. However, they are also influenced by their own personal motivations. This causes added complexity for the marketer.

Marketers may attempt to build long-term relationships with business customers to attempt to gain some advantage over their competitors.

Review Questions

1. What are the stages in the organisational buying process?
2. Who are the participants in the organisational buying process?
3. What is a product specification and why is it important in organisational buying?
4. What are the three types of organisational buying that exist?
5. How might the marketer influence the supplier selection decision?
6. What is centralised purchasing?
7. How might the gatekeeper influence the buying decision?
8. How do economic factors influence the buying decision?.

Discussion Questions

1. Apart from the use of sales people, how might a marketer provide information to participants of the decision making unit in business-to business markets?

2. Compare and contrast the factors that influence buying decisions in business markets and consumer markets.

3. Who are the people that are likely to be involved in the decision to purchase a new computer system for an office?

4. What sources is an organisational purchaser likely to consult when searching for suppliers during the buying process?

Key Terms

Buyer	Influencer	Relationship marketing
Decider	Modified rebuy	Straight rebuy
Decision making unit	New task	Supplier selection
	Partnering	User
Gatekeeper	Purchaser	

Chapter 7
Segmentation, Targeting and Positioning

Introduction

Chapters 5 and 6 indicated the complexity of buying behaviour in both consumer and business markets. You can see that it would be almost impossible for a marketer to attempt to satisfy every individual consumer or organisation. Because of this, customers with similar characteristics are grouped together. This process is known as segmentation. Think about the group of customers that buy Porsche cars. They are probably quite wealthy, belong to socio-economic grouping A or B and enjoy a 'fast' lifestyle. These characteristics define the segment or group that Porsche cars are aimed at. There would be little point in Porsche targeting other segments because they are unlikely to be able to afford the car and it may be unsuitable for their needs.

If marketers effectively identify segments, market mixes can be developed that directly match the needs of the segment. This whole process is known as **target marketing**.

Lancaster and Reynolds define segmentation as 'the process of breaking down the total market for a product or service into distinct sub groups or segments. Each segment may conceivably represent a distinct target market to be reached with a distinct marketing mix'.

The Target Marketing Process

Figure 7.1 displays the target marketing process. You can see there are three stages in this process. Each of these stages will be discussed in turn in this chapter.

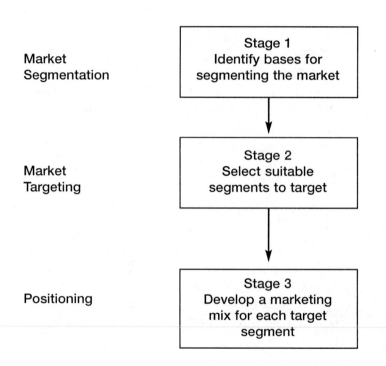

Figure 7.1 The Target Marketing Process

Stage 1: Market Segmentation

The first stage of the target marketing process involves actually identifying segments with similar characteristics; in other words, identifying suitable segmentation bases. We will deal with consumer segmentation bases and business segmentation bases separately as they are quite distinct and each of these markets is quite different in its needs and wants.

Consumer Segmentation Bases

Consumers can be segmented by a number of characteristics. The following bases are the most commonly used.

Geographic segmentation: this involves dividing markets into geographical units such as by country, by region or by town. Each geographical unit has its own distinct set of needs and wants.

Demographic segmentation: chapter 3 of this book discussed the meaning of demographics. This type of segmentation includes age, income, sex, education, family life-cycle stage, socio-economic grouping, etc. A good example of demographic segmentation in practice can be seen in consumer magazines. Magazines such as *Marie Claire* and *Vogue* are targeted at a different audience from *Take a Break* or *Woman's Own*. Hotels also segment their markets using demographic variables. Posthouses are associated with business travellers. Chapter 5 of this guide discusses the family life cycle and socio-economic groupings in some detail.

Psychographic segmentation: this involves dividing consumers into different groups on the basis of lifestyle and personality. It is concerned with how the consumer spends time, his interests and his opinions on such things as politics, social issues, education, etc. Nutrigrain is a cereal bar that is targeted at consumers with a busy lifestyle who need food on the go. Figure 7.2 lists the characteristics that are often used in psychographics segmentation.

Behavioural segmentation: This type of segmentation is associated with the types of benefits consumers seek from products, the usage rate of products and consumer loyalty to products. Consumers seek different benefits from products. Think about the car market. Some consumers want cars that offer them status, some want cars that are large enough to transport the family and others want fuel efficient cars. The example of Porsche cars discussed earlier in this chapter highlights behavioural segmentation in practice.

Marketers are also interested in the usage rate of products. It is common for organisations to target consumers that are heavy users of their products. Hilton Hotels offers a free night at their hotels for every three paying nights. This is to encourage frequent users to use the hotel even more. Consumers are often loyal to certain brands and markets can segment according to loyalty, again to encourage and retain these customers.

ACTIVITIES	INTERESTS	OPINIONS
Work	Family	Social issues
Hobbies	Home	Politics
Holidays	Job	Business
Entertainment	Recreation	Economics
Community	Food	Products
Shopping	Media	Culture
Sports	Achievements	Education

Figure 7.2 Pyschographic Segmentation in Practice

Figure 7.3 gives an overview of the bases that the marketer might consider. These bases can be used individually but in reality they are often used in combination. The better defined the market segment, the better able the marketer is to satisfy it. It is relatively easy, using both secondary and primary research, to gather information on the variables used in segmentation

Consumer Segmentation Bases	Examples of companies/products that use these bases
GEOGRAPHIC	
Country	Nescafe coffee varies in taste according to country
Region	Beer/lager is differently priced throughout the UK
Type of area	Harvey Nichols open stores in affluent areas
DEMOGRAPHIC	
Age	Ladybird clothing for children, Saga Holidays
Sex	Magazines: *Vogue, Loaded*
Race	Cosmetics: No 7, Clarins
Religion	Food manufacturers: Hallal meat
Family Life Cycle	Cars: Renault Espace for people with children
PSYCHOGRAPHIC	
Lifestyle	Filo-fax, Calvin Klein perfume
Personality	Newspaper: *Guardian , Sun, Telegraph*
BEHAVIOURAL	
Benefits sought	Many car manufacturers
Usage rate	Hilton Hotels
Customer Loyalty	Supermarket loyalty cards

Figure 7.3 An Overview of Consumer Segmentation Bases

Organisational Segmentation Bases

The same principles that applied to consumer markets also apply to business markets. Again, the marketer uses segmentation bases to identify groups with similar needs and wants within the business arena. Such segmentation bases include the following:

Geographical: segmentation by country or by region. Many organisations concentrate on individual countries or regions. Duke's Transport specialises in distributing products throughout Europe.

Type of application: this focuses on the way in which organisations might use products. Heinz might use aluminium for packaging while another company might use aluminium as an integral part of the product. This allows the marketer to develop specialisation in the end use of the product being sold.

Type of customer: markets can be segmented according to whether they are public or private institutions. They will exhibit different buying characteristics according to whether they are profit making or not.

Customer size: it is possible to target organisations according to their size. This might be measured in terms of profit or number of employees. A telecoms company might target only larger companies that have the ability to pay for its services.

Purchasing procedures: different approaches might be taken to companies with centralised purchasing departments as opposed to decentralised purchasing departments.

Benefits sought: as with consumer markets, organisational markets can be segmented according to the benefits sought by the customer.

Segmenting organisational markets is vital. There are typically fewer organisational customers than consumers and the marketer needs to understand customers if they are to be satisfied.

In both consumer and organisational segmentation, there are many bases that can be considered. However, the marketer must be sure that the identified segments are viable and useful. Some segments may be too small or inaccessible for the marketer and so will be ineffective. Effective segments should be:

◆ **S**ubstantial: the segment should be large enough and profitable enough to be targeted.

◆ **A**ccessible: the marketer must be able to reach and serve the segment. It must be possible to communicate with customers in the segment.

◆ **M**easurable: it should be relatively easy to measure the number of potential customers within each segment.

◆ **M**eaningful: the segment should be distinct in terms of specific needs that the marketer can satisfy.

Having followed the first stage of the target marketing process, the marketer should now have identified a list of possible segments to target. Each of these segments must be substantial, accessible, measurable and meaningful (SAMM). However, simply identifying potential segments is insufficient. The marketer must now select the segment(s) that will be targeted.

Stage 2: Market Targeting

Before selecting segments, the marketer must decide whether to pursue a differentiated marketing or concentrated marketing strategy.

Differentiated marketing involves targeting several segments, but offering each segment a different marketing mix. Ford operates a differentiated marketing strategy. It offers the smaller Ford Fiesta for customers seeking economy and the Ford Mondeo for those likely to be doing more driving.

Concentrated marketing involves targeting one segment only. Rolls Royce operates a concentrated marketing strategy selling cars to customers who are affluent and lead a wealthy lifestyle.

A firm that neither differentiates nor concentrates is said to operate an undifferentiated marketing strategy, attempting to sell goods and services to the masses. This type of marketing is very uncommon.

Whether differentiating or concentrating, the marketer must select suitable market segment(s) to target. The following criteria might be considered.

Segment size: is the segment large enough to offer profits that are in line with the marketer's objectives? Many segments may be profitable but it is essential that profit levels are high enough to justify entry to the market.

Segment growth: is the segment growing, declining or stable? A profitable but declining market may not be attractive because a large amount of resources must be invested to enter it. If profit can only be achieved in the short term, the investment of resources may not be considered worthwhile.

Competition: what competitors exist within this segment? The segment may be profitable and growing but may be sufficiently serviced already. The marketer may carry out a structural analysis of the market using Porter's Five Forces (see Chapter 3) to assess its attractiveness.

Company capability: does the marketer have the resources (money, staff, expertise, time) to enter the market? Some segments may appear attractive but require excessive investment.

Company objectives and image: does the segment 'fit' the overall image and objectives of the company? It may not be compatible for a company such as Harrods to begin to target less affluent consumers.

Segments should be evaluated using the above criteria. Again, this stage of the process requires secondary, and perhaps primary, research. Once the segment(s) to target have been identified the marketer can develop a positioning strategy.

Stage 3: Positioning

For each segment selected, the company must determine its product positioning strategy. Positioning relates to the way customers perceive competing products. Perhaps the easiest way to explain this is through the use of some examples. Daz powder is positioned as a powder that gets clothes white while Bold offers freshness and softness. Crest is positioned as a toothpaste that helps achieve healthy teeth and gums while Colgate keeps teeth white. So, positioning is concerned with customers perceptions, impressions and feelings about products that are competing.

It is important, therefore, for the marketer to develop a positioning strategy. One tool for doing this is by developing a positioning map. Positioning maps involve the following steps:

◆ identifying competitors that service the segment(s)

◆ identifying product attributes that customers consider important

◆ identifying competitors' position in the segment(s)

◆ selecting a position to occupy.

Figure 7.4 provides a hypothetical positioning map. Four competitors have been identified (A, B, C, D) and the product attributes that customers consider important are price and quality The competitors' position, related to these attributes, has been marked on the positioning map. The organisation wishing to enter this segment of the market can now select a position to occupy.

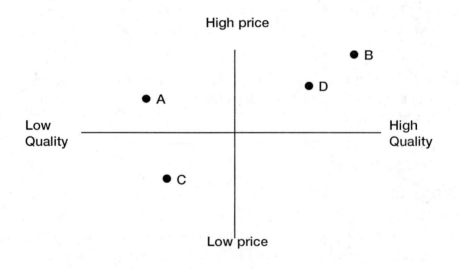

Figure 7.4 Hypothetical Positioning Map

The organisation may decide to position itself with medium prices and medium quality as there seems to be a gap in the market here. It may think about positioning itself as a high quality, low price operator. Alternatively, it may position itself as a high price, high quality operator and compete directly with companies B and D.

Once the organisation has selected a position for its products within the market place, it can use the marketing mix elements to communicate with potential customers and to confirm its position in the market.

Summary

Target marketing is a process that is used to identify customer groups so that specific marketing mixes can be used to satisfy their needs and wants. It is a three staged process consisting of segmentation, market targeting and positioning.

Consumer segmentation bases include geographic, demographic, psychographic and behavioural variables. Organisational segmentation bases include geographic, type of application and customer size. These bases are used to identify possible segments to target, but, to be effective, segments must be substantial, accessible, measurable and meaningful (SAMM).

Once possible segments have been identified, the marketer should decide whether to operate a concentrated, differentiated or undifferentiated approach. If concentrating on differentiating, segments must be assessed for their suitability. The marketer might consider market growth rate, profitability and company resources and capability.

When the segments have been selected, the organisation must position itself, relative to competitors, in the minds of consumers. A positioning map might be used at this stage.

Once the target marketing process is complete, the organisation can develop suitable marketing mixes for the segment. Management of the marketing mix is discussed in the following chapters.

Review Questions
1. What is target marketing?
2. What are the key stages in the target marketing process?
3. List the bases that might be used to segment consumer markets.
4. List the bases that might be used to segment organisational markets.
5. What does accessibility mean in relation to segmentation?
6. Explain the terms differentiated and concentrated marketing.
7. List and explain the criteria that might be used in selecting suitable market segments to target.
8. What is positioning?

Discussion Questions
1. List the characteristics of the segments that the following products may be targeted at:

    -McDonald's

    -Coca-Cola

    -Jaguar cars

    -BT

    -Microsoft
2. Identify companies that use the family lifecycle as the means for segmenting markets. Why do you think this segmentation base was used?
3. Explain the segmentation bases used in the consumer toothpaste market.
4. Some companies target both consumer and organisational markets. Identify two companies that operate in this way and list the segmentation bases they might have used to identify suitable segments.

5. You are thinking about opening a new clothing store targeting 18-30 year old affluent men. Draw a positioning map to aid your positioning decision.

Key Terms

Accessible	Meaningful	Segmentation bases
Behavioural segmentation	Measurable	Substantial
Concentrated marketing	Positioning	Target market
Demographic segmentation	Positioning map	Targeting
Differentiated marketing	Product attributes	Undifferentiated marketing
Geographic segmentation	Psychographic segmentation	

Chapter 8
Product

Introduction

The concept of the marketing mix has already been introduced in Chapter 2 of this book, the elements being product, price, place and promotion (the 4 Ps). The marketing mix is the means used by the marketer to satisfy customers. In this chapter we look at the product element of the marketing mix.

The product is the item or object that the marketer offers to a market. It is important to realise that a product might be a tangible offering such as a car or a stereo or it might be an intangible offering (a service) such as hairdressing or financial services. This is made more complex by the fact that many companies sell tangible products with accompanying services. Car dealers may offer services such as financing, free servicing and warranties.

So, a product might be seen as anything the marketer offers to customers to satisfy a need or a want. This means that the marketer is not simply selling a product; he is selling a 'bundle of satisfactions'. See Figure 8.1.

Pure services marketing has additional considerations and so this area will be discussed in more detail in Chapter 12 of this book.

The Product Defined

Because the marketer is selling a 'bundle of satisfactions', products can be viewed on three levels. Figure 8.1 displays these three levels.

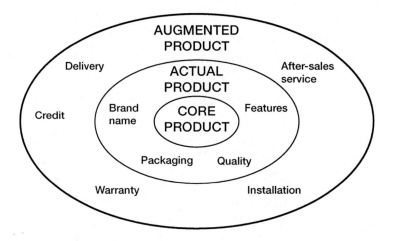

Figure 8.1 Three Levels of a Product
(adapted from Marketing, Kotler and Armstrong)

Level 1: The Core Product

This relates to the benefit sought by a customer when buying a product. For example, an individual buys a car so that he or she can be mobile. Therefore, the core product or benefit satisfies the customers core need – the need for mobility.

Level 2: The Actual Product

The actual product is built around the core product. It consists of those elements that make the core product physical. If we think about our car example again, it is the car's features, brand name, the quality of manufacture and styling which make the product physical or actual. It is also these elements that allow the marketer to differentiate his product offering from those of his competitors. The marketer has many options when deciding on the actual product:

Quality level: the product may be high or low quality. This has a direct impact on other elements of the marketing mix. For instance, pricing and promotion are directly affected by the quality of a product.

Features: a product may be basic or incorporate many additional features. In the case of a car, added features might include power steering, sun roof, air conditioning, etc. Again, the features of a product have a direct impact on other elements of the marketing mix. When deciding on features, the marketing department should work closely with other departments such as engineering, production and R & D.

Brand name: deciding the brand name and image is crucial. The brand often communicates the entire product image to potential customers. Think about the difference in image of a Vauxhall Tigra and the VW Beetle. The Tigra brand name suggests a fast, aggressive car while the Beetle brand name suggests a fun car.

Packaging: packaging might also be significant to the customer – particularly in consumer markets. Cosmetics companies recognise the importance of packaging to their customers. Think about the packaging of Clinique products.

Level 3: The Augmented Product

This relates to the additional services and benefits that might be offered with the core and actual product. If you were buying a photocopier for your office, you might expect a guaranteed delivery time and date, installation, after sales servicing and a free warranty. Again, many marketers use the augmented product to differentiate their product offerings from competitors.

Figure 8.1 indicates the complexities involved in product decisions. A marketing orientated company is unlikely to make a product and sell it. The company will consider all elements of the product so that customer needs can be satisfied.

Product decisions impact directly on other elements of the marketing mix. Low quality products are unlikely to be sold at high prices. Unique brands are likely to be distributed selectively and the entire promotional message will be influenced by the product and its features. So, product decisions must not be taken in isolation.

Additionally, product decisions impact on other areas of the organisation. If the marketer wishes to change any features of the product then it might be necessary to consult with:

◆ the R & D department to see whether the new features can be incorporated into the product

◆ the production department to ensure the product can be manufactured

◆ the accounts department to ensure the cost of the new features will not erode profits

◆ the sales department to inform them of the benefits of the new features.

Marketing decisions cannot be taken in isolation. They impact on all areas of a business.

Brand Management

Branding is part of the actual product and is a major issue in overall product strategy. Branding is used to give products unique identities and is a tool used by the marketer to differentiate their products from those of competitors. Additionally, marketers may benefit from the fact that customers may become brand loyal.

In the UK, the supermarkets have recognised the benefits of branding. Both Tesco and Sainsburys are extending their ranges of own-brand merchandise everyday. Consumers are beginning to trust these brands more and more. Many retailers create 'reseller' brands. Marks & Spencer has relied on this branding strategy for years. M&S sources products from manufacturers and the manufacturers print the M&S brand onto packaging and labelling. M&S retains control of how the products/brands are marketed and sold.

A brand is not simply a name. A brand incorporates the logo, symbols and design as well as the name. Think about Nike, the sportswear manufacturer. The Nike brand includes the name, the italic design of the name, the 'swoosh' and the logo 'just do it!'. It is each of these factors which gives Nike its unique identity.

Branding offers many advantages:

◆ Customers know and recognise brands and so they do not have to go through a lengthy decision making process (see Chapters 5 and 6) every time they make a buying decision.

◆ It encourages customer loyalty and therefore helps to increase profits. Many customers will request products by their brand names.

◆ It helps in the design of advertising and other promotional activities.

◆ It allows the marketer to charge higher prices because customers perceive brands as higher value.

◆ It helps with the segmentation process.

◆ It helps the marketer to build a corporate image.

◆ It helps when launching new products. Customers are more likely to try a new product with a brand name they recognise.

◆ A brand has a financial value and can be viewed as an asset to an organisation.

However, branding does add cost. Brands must be legally protected and packaging must be designed to incorporate the brand. Also, marketers face high risks if the brand is not successful with customers. Volkswagen is investing large amounts of money to try to eradicate the image that many customers have of the Skoda brand.

Figure 8.2 indicates the steps involved in developing a brand once the decision to brand has been taken.

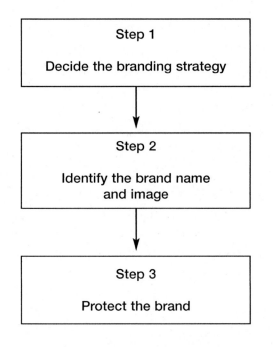

Figure 8.2 The Branding Process

Step 1: Decide the Branding Strategy

There are three main types of branding strategy.

Corporate branding: this means that a company uses its own company name as a brand for its products. Examples of corporate branding include Nike, Microsoft and IBM. This type of branding strategy offers the advantage of lower costs in design and marketing and, because customers are familiar with the brand name, they may try any new products launched under the brand. It also helps a company to build a global image. However, there are dangers associated with corporate branding. The failure of one product may be detrimental to the entire organisation.

Family branding: this involves using a brand image and name for a range of products. An example of this might be the Lean Cuisine range of food products. Again, because the brand name exists, launch costs of new products may be low and brand loyal customers are more likely to try the branded new products.

Individual branding: this means that each product is given a distinct name and image by a company. Nestlé uses individual branding quite successfully. Nestlé brands include Kit Kat, After Eights, Yorkie, Quality Street, Aero, Rolo and Smarties. Individual branding means that if one brand fails, it is unlikely to damage the reputation of other brands.

Step 2: Identify the Brand Name and Image

Actually selecting a brand name can be very difficult. There are numerous examples of companies that have got it wrong. For instance, in China, the Kentucky Fried Chicken slogan 'finger-lickin good' translated as 'eat your fingers off'. In Taiwan, the translation of the Pepsi slogan 'Come alive with the Pepsi Generation' translated as 'Pepsi will bring your ancestors back from the dead'. In Italy, a campaign for Schweppes Tonic Water translated into Schweppes Toilet Water. Brand names should be easy to pronounce, easy to recognise and easy to remember. Once the name has been selected the design and colouring can be decided so that the brand's unique identity can be developed.

Step 3: Protect the Brand

If the brand is unique, the marketer can legally protect the name against imitation through trade marking. A trade mark is a legal term covering words and symbols that can be registered and protected.

Even with legal protection, many companies suffer from imitations of their products. You might have seen 'fake' Levi jeans and Nike shoes. These imitations can be detrimental to overall brand image and can erode some of the potential profits to companies that have invested large sums of money in brand development.

The Product Lifecycle

Deciding the product mix is only one aspect of managing the product element of the marketing mix. The product itself, as well as the other elements of the marketing mix, must be managed through the entire product lifecycle.

The product lifecycle (PLC) is a model that displays the sales of any product (or service) over a period of time. Figure 8.3 shows a typical product lifecycle. You can see from this figure that the amount of sales achieved by a product typically change over a period of time. Perhaps the easiest way to explain the PLC concept is through the use of an example. When mobile phones were first launched onto the market, sales were relatively low. They were expensive and not as reliable as they are now. Typically, they were used only by business people. As reliability increased and prices came down, more and more people began to buy mobile phones. Therefore, sales began to grow. Currently, mobile phones are selling well. There are perhaps more sales of mobile phones than ever before – as indicated by the X on the graph. Sales of mobile phones are expected to decrease in coming years (indicated by the dotted line) as there are fewer people left without one. Also, new products may come onto the market that supersede mobile phones. You might also consider the PLC in the context of a particular model of mobile phone. Nokia, for example, is continually introducing new and improved models, thus encouraging replacement purchases.

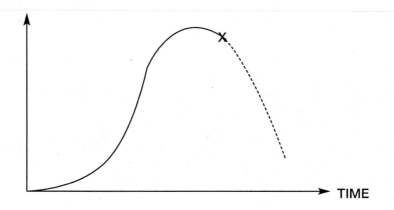

Figure 8.3 Typical Sales of Mobile Phones

The PLC displayed in Figure 8.3 displays a limited amount of information in its current state. To make it useful, the marketer typically divides the PLC into four main stages as identified in Figure 8.4. Each of these stages has characteristics associated with it and, the marketer is better able to make marketing mix decisions that suit each stage of the PLC. Each stage will be discussed in some detail.

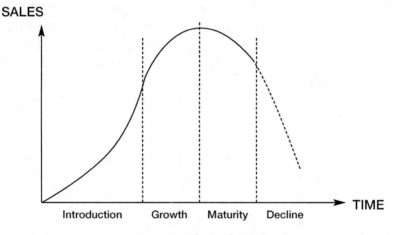

Figure 8.4 The Product Lifecycle

Introduction

When a product is launched onto the market, sales are likely to be slow. This is mainly because customers are unaware of the new product or are wary of buying something new. So, sales are low. Unfortunately, costs for a company at this stage of the PLC are high. The company has probably invested large amounts of money to develop and launch the product and,so, is unlikely to be making profit at this time.

Growth

During the growth stage, more customers begin to buy the product. This could be because customers who purchased during the introduction stage are repeat purchasing or have recommended the product to colleagues, friends and family. Sales will begin to grow and the company should begin to make a profit. At this stage, competitors may enter the market.

Maturity

Sales of the product reach their optimum level at maturity stage and, typically, sales growth slows down. Companies may experience high profits at the maturity stage because sales levels are high but costs are low (because of economies of scale). Competition is at its height in the maturity stage and so companies will compete to retain market share.

Decline

At this stage, sales of the product begin to fall. This is usually because a new product has become available that better satisfies the customer's need. Companies typically attempt to reduce costs at this stage.

It is probably useful for you to think about a product that has gone through an entire PLC. For example, John Grisham's book *The Client* has now reached the decline stage of the PLC.

Figure 8.5 overviews the characteristics associated with each stage of the PLC.

Stage			
Introduction	**Growth**	**Maturity**	**Decline**
Low sales	Increasing sales	Peak sales	Sales fall
High cost	Costs decrease	Lowest costs	Low costs
Financial losses	Profits rise	Optimum profits	Profits fall
Few customers	Increased number of customers	Mass market	Decreased number of customers
Few competitors	More competitors	Stable number of competitors	Less competitors

Figure 8.5 Characteristics of PLC

Managing the Marketing Mix

The PLC is a strategic tool that is used by marketers to help make marketing mix decisions. Because certain characteristics are associated with each stage of the PLC (see Figure 8.5), the marketing mix is likely to change at each stage. If we look at each stage of the PLC in turn, we can see how the marketing mix might change. At this stage of the book, we will not look at the other mix elements in depth. However, as you read the preceding chapters, you should keep the PLC in mind.

Introduction

Because the organisation is typically making a loss during the introduction stage, it will encourage customers to try the product. The company is likely to use promotions to encourage product trial and to build product awareness. Additionally, because the product is new, it is likely to be basic without many additional features. At the introduction stage, the marketer has two pricing options: skimming and penetration. Skimming involves pricing the product high to recover some of the development costs. Penetration pricing involves launching the product at a relatively low cost to encourage many customers to try the product. At this stage, the product is likely to be concentrated on a few key outlets. Distributors may not be willing to stock the product until it is in the growth stage of the PLC.

Growth

At this stage, competitors are entering the market and so the marketer will attempt to encourage customers, through promotion, to remain loyal to his brand/product. Pricing may remain quite static at the growth phase but the marketer will search for new distributors to increase the level of market penetration.

Maturity

At this stage, the product will be improved and new features will, perhaps, be added to it. Indeed, additional product lines may be introduced at this stage (think about Mars miniatures and Mars ice creams). Pricing will match or beat the competition and promotion will be used to encourage customers to switch from competing brands. Distribution will be intensified where possible. A good example of this can be seen with mobile phones. Mobile phones are now distributed through music shops and supermarkets.

Decline

Because sales are decreasing at the decline stage, marketers will spend less on the other elements of the marketing mix. Usually, prices are decreased at this stage and distribution is phased out. Marketers may launch new products.

Figure 8.6 overviews the marketing mix at each stage of the PLC. However, this is a guideline only. Marketing mix decisions are more complex than highlighted here.

	INTRODUCTION	GROWTH	MATURITY	DECLINE
Product	Basic product	Improve basic product	Add product features and generate new product lines	Rationalise product range and launch new products
Price	Price skimming or penetration	Price to increase sales	Match or beat the competition	Lower price
Place	Building distribution network	Find new outlets	Build more intensive distribution	Rationalise outlets
Promotion	Promote to encourage trial	Build brand image	Emphasis brand strengths	Minmal levels

Figure 8.6 The Marketing Mix and the PLC

The PLC is useful for the marketer. However, it is a rather simplistic approach. When using the PLC the marketer should be aware of the following drawbacks:

◆ The PLC depicts sales, not profits or costs.
◆ The PLC can only be plotted after sales have occurred, therefore any planning is based on forecasting and estimating.
◆ It is difficult to ascertain which stage of the PLC a product has actually reached. Figure 8.4 indicates a very smooth sales line. However, in reality, sales will go through minor peaks and troughs. Therefore, a marketer might misread a minor trough as the onslaught of decline. Marketing mix decisions might then be taken that encourage decline.
◆ Not all products follow the typical bell-shaped PLC.
◆ A PLC must be developed for each of the organisation's products.
◆ It does not really consider the competitive position or the PEST factors.

So the PLC should not be used in isolation when making marketing mix decisions. Another useful tool is the Boston Consulting Group (BCG) matrix (see Figure 8.7).

The Boston Consulting Group Matrix

The BCG matrix considers market share and market growth rate and all of an organisation's products might be displayed on one matrix. A company would plot its major products in the appropriate cells of the matrix to gain an overview of how the entire portfolio of products was performing.

The market growth rate axis indicates the attractiveness and profit potential of a market. A market that is growing and expanding is perhaps more attractive than a market that is stable or growing relatively slowly.

The market share axis is a measure of how successful a company's products are in that market. It relates to the amount of sales a company makes, relative to its competitors. Generally, the higher the market share, the more cash a product will generate.

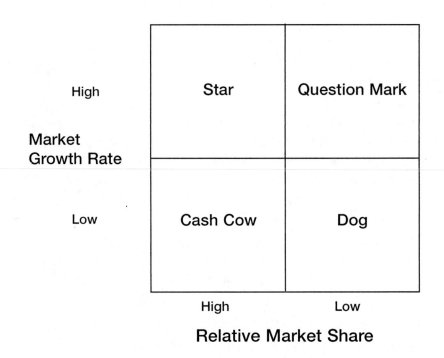

Figure 8.7 The BCG Matrix

Stars

Products are classified as stars when the market growth rate is high and the products command a high level of market share. In other words, the organisation is achieving high sales in this market and, the market is continuing to grow. Stars often required high levels of investment to maintain their growth. However, this investment is justified because they may eventually become cash cows.

Cash Cows

Products that achieve high market share in a relatively low growth market are classified as cash cows. These products are usually very profitable because they do not require high levels of financial investment and because they are usually at the maturity stage of the PLC.

Question Marks

Question marks, sometimes known as problem children, are products that are in high growth markets but are achieving low levels of market share. They require significant investment if they are to achieve higher levels of market share. The company must think seriously about whether to invest further in these products. If successful, a question mark could be turned into a star. However, investing in question marks is risky. If they do not achieve higher levels of market share, they will simply be a drain on resources.

Dogs

These products have low market share in a low growth rate market. Dogs are not always loss making but they can be a drain on resources. A dog that is also in the decline phase of the PLC should be discontinued.

You can see that the BCG matrix provides the marketing planner with more detailed information with which to make strategic decisions. It considers the company's competitive position as well as the market as a whole. It also provides the company with information about its total product portfolio. If a company has many dogs, it may wish to look for new products or new markets. Likewise, too many stars may result in an overburden of cost for the company.

New Product Development

Any organisation that wishes to survive long term, must invest in new product development (NPD). Almost all products eventually reach the decline stage of the PLC. Without new products, an organisation's sales will eventually become non-existent. Customers will seek competitors' products. Additionally, by introducing new and innovative products to the market place first, an organisation may generate customer loyalty and maintain its market share as the market grows.

NPD is costly and can be a long process. Figure 8.8 indicates a typical NPD process. Each of the stages of the process will be discussed in turn. Launching new products is a risky business. If a new product fails, a company may make huge financial losses and the ensuing bad publicity can be detrimental. The NPD process helps to minimise the risk of failure. Ideas and products are tested and analysed at each stage of the process in an attempt to minimise the rise of an unsuccessful product launch.

Idea Generation

Idea generation should be a constant activity in any organisation. It is ideas that are eventually made into profitable products and services. Ideas for new products can come from many sources including staff, customers, suppliers and competitors. Many companies now offer incentives to their staff for identifying new product ideas. Idea generation should not be an ad hoc activity. To launch new products onto the market is essential for the long-term survival of a company. Therefore, generating ideas should be encouraged on an ongoing basis.

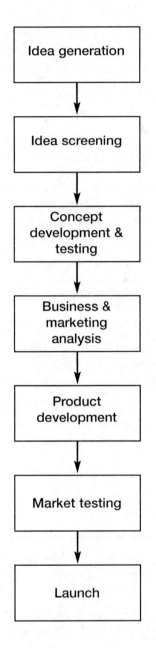

Figure 8.8 The NPD Process

Idea Screening

Many of the ideas generated for new products will not be suitable for a company. The purpose of screening ideas is to reduce the number of ideas to those that have potential. In order to screen out unsuitable ideas, a company might consider such things as:

◆ Does the product fit with our current portfolio?

◆ Is the image of the product compatible with the corporate image?

◆ Is it easy to manufacture?

◆ Do we have the financial capability to develop the product?

◆ Is it better than, or different from, competitors' offerings?

Each stage of the NPD process is more expensive and time consuming than the previous one. It is important at this stage to 'weed out' ideas without potential.

Concept Development and Testing

Once the ideas have been screened, it is time to develop and test a concept for each idea. A concept is a detailed overview of the idea. This is perhaps easier to explain through the use of an example. Say a company had the idea of new type of snack bar that was high in Vitamin C, then this idea (the snack) might have several concepts:

Concept 1: High vitamin snack suitable for children's lunches.

Concept 2: High vitamin snack to give athlete's energy.

Concept 3: High vitamin snack for the elderly or sick.

Concept 4: High vitamin snack suitable for pregnant women.

You can see that from one single idea, several concepts have been developed. Each of these concepts relates to the potential target customers. At this stage, the product is still not tangible. However, in order to take the idea further, some kind of testing is required to check whether the product would be attractive to customers.

Concept testing can be done with potential customers through the use of graphics and explanations, or through actual physical product development. Whichever method is used, it is important to assess customer response to the concept and the product. Customers can be asked for their opinions about the new product and the likelihood that they will buy it. Again, ideas and concepts without potential can be eliminated at this stage of the process.

Business and Marketing Analysis

It is now time to look at the commercial viability of the product. Much research will be performed at this stage to check the cost and profit potential of the product idea and concept.

The company will check sources and costs of supply, likely costs of manufacture and/or distribution, advertising costs, marketing costs and other associated costs. It will also endeavour to carry out some form of sales forecasting to aid with profit projections. Again, ideas without potential will be eliminated at this stage. To date, the NPD process has been relatively inexpensive (see Figure 8.9). However, the next stage (product development) will involve high costs. It is important that products without commercial viability are eliminated now.

Product Development

The concept and idea is now developed into a physical product. This may involve many departments within the organisation. R&D will be involved in the design, production in actually making it, finance in costing, marketing in designing and developing packaging, etc. The company may develop a limited number of prototypes for market testing. Alternatively, once the prototype is error free, the company may go into full scale production to launch the product.

Market Testing

This is said to be the only optional part of the NPD process. It involves a 'real-life' test of the new product so that it might be improved before a full scale launch. Many organisations avoid market testing as it involves cost and provides competitors with information about new products before a full scale launch.

Market testing can be done in many ways. For industrial or business-to-business products, a company may ask loyal customers to trial the product and provide feedback. For consumer products, a full scale test marketing programme may ensue.

Test marketing is one form of market testing. It involves a 'mini launch' of the new product. Usually, a region is selected and the product is launched. Northern Ireland is often used as a test market for consumer products. The product is launched to the test market and it is backed up by advertising and other forms of promotion. Through this miniature launch a company can gain information on:

overall costs

amount of advertising required

distributor requirements

optimum selling price

◆ projected sales volumes

typical customer profiles

manufacturing requirements.

Test marketing reduces the risk of failure of a full launch. It also enables the company to 'fine tune' the final version of the product and to solve any problem areas. However, there are various problems with test marketing:

It alerts competitors to company plans.

It is costly.

Economies of scale may not be achieved because of shorter production runs.

◆ There is a missed profit opportunity. If the test marketing programme ran for six months and proved successful, the organisation has missed out on six months of full profits from a full launch.

◆ Management time is used in monitoring the test market.

Launch

This is the final stage in the NPD process. The product is launched onto the market. Costs at this stage are high. An overview of the costs associated with NPD can be seen in Figure 8.9.

A launch is often supported by significant promotional activity. However, once launched, the product enters the introduction stage of the PLC and, by growth or maturity, should be reclaiming the costs associated with developing it, and providing profits for the company. The PLC and BCG matrix can then be used to develop the marketing strategy for the rest of the product's selling life.

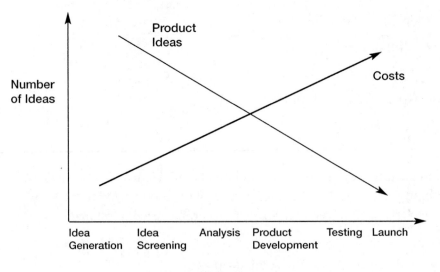

Figure 8.9 Costs of NPD process

Once launched onto the market, customers will, hopefully, purchase the product. However, customers do not purchase goods as soon as they become available. Some of us will buy new, innovative goods. Others will wait until the goods have been available on the market for some time before we buy them. This process is known as the diffusion of innovations – the rate at which we adopt or try new product. Figure 8.10 overviews the product adoption process.

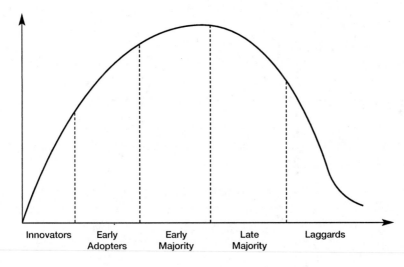

Figure 8.10 The Product Adoption Process (Everett Rogers)

When new products are launched, innovators are likely to trial (adopt) the product relatively quickly. Innovators are likely to be relatively affluent and broad-minded.

The next type of people likely to buy new products are early adopters. Early adopters are often opinion leaders and tend to exercise a lot of influence on their friends and family's buying behaviour (see Chapter 5).

Once new products have been accepted by the innovators and early adopters, the majority of people tend to buy them. The early and late majority are reassured by the fact the innovators have accepted the new products and have listened to information about the product.

The last group of adopters are known as laggards. This is the most cautious group of individuals. Laggards tend to be older with less income and so tend to buy later than other groups of people.

Summary

This chapter has given you some detail about the extent of product management. There are three levels to any product: the core product, the actual product and the augmented product: Each level of the product can be changed or improved to gain competitive advantage.

Branding is one means of achieving competitive advantage. Branding can be costly. However, a successful branding strategy helps a company to ensure customer loyalty.

Almost all products go through a product lifecycle consisting of introduction, growth, maturity and decline. The PLC is a tool which aids the marketer in developing marketing strategy. However, the PLC should be used in conjunction with other analytical tools such as the BCG matrix if it is to be meaningful.

Because sales of products eventually decline, it is important for companies to constantly develop new products. The NPD process can be time consuming and costly, but it does reduce the risk of failure of new products.

Review Questions

1. What are the three product levels?
2. Why do marketers consider the product on three levels?
3. What is the PLC?
4. What is the purpose of the PLC?

5. List three criticisms of the PLC.

6. Draw the BCG matrix.

7. What is the purpose of the BCG matrix?

8. What are the characteristics of a cash cow?

9. List the steps involved in the NPD process.

10. Why do companies constantly need to develop new product ideas?

11. Explain the concept of test marketing as part of the NPD process.

12. What does 'diffusion of innovation' mean?

Discussion Questions

1. How might a company that sells services use the NPD process?

2. What stage of the PLC do you think each of the following products are at:

    -Dyson vacuum cleaners

    -Mars Bars

    -The internet

    -Gas/electricity

3. 'The PLC is a useful planning tool. However, it cannot be used in isolation'. Discuss.

4. 'Test marketing is a waste of resources'. Discuss.

5. Recommend a marketing strategy for an industrial product of your choice at the maturity stage of the PLC.

Key Terms

Actual product	Dog	Late majority
Augmented product	Early adopters	Market growth rate
BCG matrix	Early majority	Market share
Branding	Family branding	Maturity
Cash cow	Growth	NPD process
Core product	Individual branding	Product lifecycle
Corporate branding	Innovators	Question mark
Decline	Introduction	Star
Diffusion of innovation	Laggards	

Chapter 9
Price

Introduction

Pricing is a key issue for any organisation. Pricing is the only element of the marketing mix that actually generates money. If a product is priced too high, customers may not purchase it. If a product is priced too low, profit margins will also be low. Getting the price of a product or service wrong may result in low profits or even losses.

In this chapter we look at pricing from a marketing perspective. Traditionally, pricing has been associated with the accounting function. From an accounting perspective, costs of a product must be recovered through the selling price. So, calculating the price and adding a mark-up ensures that an organisation makes a profit on each unit of sale. However, this approach is not customer orientated. Customers are often willing to pay higher prices for branded or exclusive goods. Simply adding a mark-up to costs means that a product may not achieve its profit potential. Pricing can help with the positioning strategy (see Chapter 7).

Influences on the Pricing Decision

We have already introduced the concept that costs are not the only influence on a pricing decision. Having said this, it is essential, at least in the longer term, to achieve a profit. Costs should be covered. Costs include factors such as raw materials, energy, labour, packaging, rent and rates, equipment, etc.

Demand is also an important influence on the pricing decision. Demand relates to sales of a product at a given price. Information on demand can be gathered through marketing research and test marketing. A typical demand curve is displayed in Figure 9.1. From this figure you can see that as price decreases, demand rises. So, it displays the effect on demand of changes in price, i.e. the price elasticity.

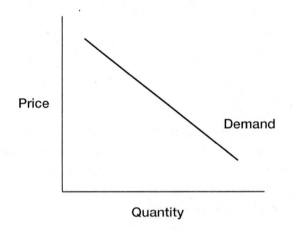

Figure 9.1 Demand Curve

The steeper a demand curve, the less sensitive demand is to changes in price; the price is inelastic. The flatter a demand curve, the more sensitive demand is to changes in price; the price is elastic. Figure 9.2 displays inelastic and elastic demand curves. You can see that there is little change in the quantity demanded (b) when price is reduced (a) in an inelastic situation. However, there is a significant change in quantity demanded (b) when price is reduced (a) in an elastic situation.

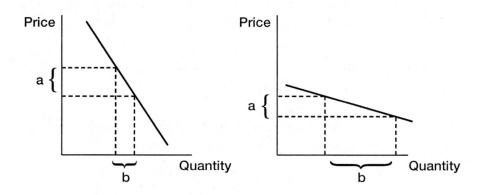

Figure 9.2 Elasticity

Simply calculating demand and elasticity of demand is perhaps too straightforward. There are many more influences on the pricing decision and elasticity. They are:

Stage in the product life cycle: a product is likely to be priced differently throughout the PLC. Mobile phones are now much cheaper than they used to be. This might be related to the PLC. Mobile phones are at the maturity stage. Many people have bought or are buying mobile phones and communications companies are benefiting from economies of scale in production and marketing. Therefore, prices have fallen. If the product is also a 'cash cow', the company can afford to drop prices because of the limited amount of investment required to sustain profitability (see Chapter 8).

Corporate and marketing objectives: if a company is seeking market share then it is likely to set prices a low as possible. If it is seeking profit maximisation, then price elasticity will become more important.

The product portfolio: a product is likely to be priced so that it 'fits in' with other products in a company's portfolio. For instance, almost all Nike products are likely to be premium priced to maintain the brand image. If a company has several different brands in its product portfolio, it may chose to price each brand at a different level. For instance, Unilever sells both Persil and Surf washing powder. Persil is relatively highly priced while Surf is priced at the lower end of the spectrum.

Target market: the characteristics of the target market affect the pricing decision. In consumer markets, if the target market has high levels of disposable income, a company may charge high prices for its products. In business-to-business markets, the amount of potential customers may be small, so a company may be forced to charge higher prices.

Competition: if a company faces high levels of competition it may be forced to lower prices. Alternatively, if it is one of a limited source of supply, a company may have more freedom to raise prices.

Customer perception: if customers perceive products to be of high quality or exclusive image, a company may be able to charge premium prices. Rolls Royce cars are expensive, yet customers are willing to pay the price. This relates to the perception of the image and quality of the cars from a customer perspective.

State of the economy: if the economy is in recession, consumers have less disposable income. If the economy is booming, consumers have more disposable income. This affects the prices of both consumer and business/industrial goods.

Distribution: many companies do not sell directly to their customers. Instead they use intermediaries such as distributors, agents, wholesalers and/or retailers. Each intermediary will add its own mark-up to products. Therefore, the selling price is increased by the time the product reaches the customer.

Pricing Strategies for New Products

Once all of the above influences have been considered, a company can start to think about its pricing strategies. For new products being launched to the market, there are two pricing strategies: skimming and penetration.

Price skimming involves setting a high price initially, to 'skim' as much profit as possible in the early stages of the PLC. Price skimming was used by mobile phone companies at the introduction stage of the PLC. This approach is particularly suited to products that are innovative with few directly competing products. The price can then be reduced at later stages of the PLC to expand demand. Price skimming has the added benefit of portraying a quality image to potential customers and may encourage 'innovators' and 'early adapters' (see Chapter 8) to trial the product. However, a high price may also encourage competitors to enter the market because they see that profits can be achieved. Also, a high price may mean limited levels of demand. Therefore, a company may not gain economies of scale in production and marketing at the early stages of the PLC.

Price penetration is almost the opposite approach of skimming. It involves setting an initially low price. Low prices will encourage customers to purchase a product and therefore demand should increase quickly and the company should benefit from economies of scale. It also discourages competitors from entering the market because margins are low. However, there is little room for error. Customers may not be happy if they see prices rising later in the PLC.

Figure 9.3 provides an overview of the factors encouraging price skimming and penetration.

Factors Encouraging Skimming	Factors Encouraging Penetration
Prices are likely to be inelastic	Prices are likely to be elastic
The product or service is innovative/unique	Competitors are likely to enter the market quickly
Distinct target markets exist	There are no distinct target markets
Quality is important to the customer	Products are undifferentiated
Competitive costs are unknown	Economies of scale apply

Figure 9.3 (adapted from Marketing by David Mercer)

Pricing Strategies for Established Products

For products that are at later stages of the PLC a company may select premium or economy pricing.

Premium pricing involves setting high prices. The company can usually justify this because of the quality of its products and the level of service it offers. Products such as Chanel perfume and Calvin Klein clothing are sold at premium prices. Customers are often happy to pay premium prices because they perceive the products, or brands, to be of high quality.

Economy pricing as its name suggests, economy pricing involves setting relatively low prices. Supermarket chain Kwik Save operates an economy pricing strategy. The company can do this because it offers a 'no frills' shopping experience.

A company must take all pricing influences into account when deciding the pricing strategy. The price of a product communicates a message to customers. How would you feel about Porsche cars if prices were reduced so much that almost everyone could afford to buy one?

Simply deciding the pricing strategy is insufficient in actually setting the final selling price. Pricing strategy is a long-term decision. It is an approach to the market. Actually setting the final price is more complicated because a company must consider short term tactical approaches.

Pricing Tactics

The following discussion overviews the short-term tactical approaches that a company might use when pricing products. You should realise that even though a company may take a standard strategic approach, its prices may vary. For instance, you will often pay more for a glass of beer in the South of England than in the North. This is because, although the brewery uses the same pricing strategy nationwide, it also uses geographical pricing (a short-term pricing tactic). The following pricing tactics may be used:

Geographical pricing: the example above showed that prices can change throughout the UK for single products. It is widely believed that individuals in the South of England have higher levels of disposable income than in the North. Therefore many companies have different selling prices, depending on the geographical location of customers. This pricing tactic is also used internationally by many companies. Ford cars are sold at different prices throughout Europe, even though the company uses economy pricing (for most of its models).

Psychological pricing: this type of pricing is more suited to consumer markets as it involves getting customers to respond emotionally to a price. The most common method of psychological pricing is through the use of prices like £9.99 or £9,995. Logically, we know that £9.99 is only one penny less than £10.00 but, emotionally, the £9.99 price attracts us more. This pricing tactic is used in both premium and economy pricing. You can see evidence of it in car showrooms, supermarkets and on the internet.

Off-peak pricing: many companies encourage customers to buy goods at 'off-peak' rates. Perhaps the best of example of this can be seen on trains. Travel is much cheaper after 9.30 am. This is to encourage customers to travel out of peak times.

Discounts: lower prices are often offered in the short term to encourage customers to buy goods. Discounts may be given because products have reached the decline stage of the PLC or a company has discontinued the line. We get many discounts on goods during sale periods. Again, discounts can be given on economy and premium priced goods. Marks and Spencer has sale periods for its premium priced goods. New Look has sale periods for its economy priced goods.

Trade discounts: intermediaries (distributors, retailers, etc) often receive trade discounts for buying in bulk. This allows the intermediary to make higher profits, or to pass the discount on to its customers.

Loss leaders: some companies sell products at a loss. Remember, this is usually a short-term tactic. By selling products at a loss, the company generates goodwill, encourages further purchasing and takes market share. Supermarkets often use loss leaders. They will often sell products such as milk or bread at a loss in the hope that customers will purchase more products while in-store. Profit is generated from the additional purchases.

Optional feature pricing: customers are given the option of additional features on a product. Each additional feature increases the selling price of the product. This pricing tactic is often used in the car market. Features such as a sunroof, air conditioning or electric windows increase the price of a basic model.

Promotional pricing: companies often offer promotional prices to encourage sales. Products may have lower prices for certain periods.

Pricing in Industrial Markets

Many of the pricing strategies and tactics we have discussed can be used in industrial or business-to-business markets. However, because of the characteristics of such markets, approaches to pricing may differ. Remember, in these markets there are likely to be fewer customers but each sale is likely to be larger (in value). Also, companies often sell products direct to their customers rather than through intermediaries.

Business customers often place great emphasis on the augmented product. The decision to purchase may be based on the warranty, installation and servicing of equipment. In many instances, the decision to purchase may be based on a thorough product specification (see Chapter 6). Therefore, the price of a product is often negotiable depending on the terms and conditions agreed between the buyer and seller. It is also likely that the parties have an established a relationship.

In this instance, the marketer should be willing to negotiate with the customer. The selling company may have a pricing strategy in place, but the final selling price is developed through negotiation with the customer.

Many companies and organisations go through a tendering process when making purchases. Indeed, public sector organisations in the EU, by law, have to use competitive tendering when making purchases. In this case, the business customer draws up a specification and invites suppliers (sellers) to bid for the business. The specification will list all the customer's requirements. The bid that satisfies the customer's needs at the lowest price is usually accepted by the buying organisation.

It is imperative for the company to plan thoroughly if it is to be successful in competitive bidding. Hutt and Speh state that there are three important steps when planning in competitive bidding.

Step 1: Define Objectives

The industrial company or seller must carefully define its objectives. There may be many opportunities to bid, so setting objectives helps the company to decide what types of business to pursue, when to bid and how much to bid. As in consumer markets, objectives will be based on market share or profit maximisation.

Step 2: Screening Bid Opportunities

Developing bids is costly. Therefore, contracts to bid for should be carefully selected. Again, the contracts selected should fit in with the company objectives. The company must also consider the longer-term implications of the bid. It may result in repeat business and a long-term profitable relationship.

Step 3: Bidding Strategy

Once the bid has been selected, the company should estimate the probability of winning the contract at various prices (assuming the contract is awarded to the lowest bidder). So, to win the contract, the company may aim to be the lowest bidder. However, this may be difficult.

It is usually impossible to gain knowledge about competitors' bids. So simply bidding at a very low price to win a bid is not advisable (too low a price may result in lost profit opportunity). If the project is strategically important (see Step 2) then the company may bid very low.

Summary

The pricing decision is a crucial one. It may result in lost profit opportunities.

Simply considering supply and demand is insufficient. There are many other considerations when pricing a product such as costs, target market, objectives and competitors.

Once the pricing influences have been considered a company may opt for a number of pricing strategies. Price skimming or penetration can be used for new products. Economy of premium pricing can be used for established products. Yet, still the pricing decision is incomplete.

Before settling on a final selling price, a company may also consider the tactical issues associated with pricing. Within the pricing strategy it will also consider such tactics as geographic pricing, discounts, additional features, etc.

Although industrial pricing is similar to consumer pricing, the industrial company has several more considerations. In some situations, the industrial company cannot actually set the final selling price as this will be established through negotiation with the customer. In other situations, the industrial company may become involved in competitive bidding. When bidding, the lowest price usually wins the contract, therefore the industrial company must carefully consider which contracts it bids for.

Review Questions

1. Why is price such a crucial element of the marketing mix?
2. Explain price elasticity.
3. Why is elasticity not the only consideration in pricing?
4. List five other factors that influence the pricing decision.
5. What are the advantages and disadvantages of penetration pricing?
6. What are the advantages and disadvantages of price skimming?
7. Explain economy and premium pricing.
8. List and explain three pricing tactics.
9. What is competitive bidding?

Discussion Questions

1. When a company introduces a new product, how should it decide

between a skimming and penetration price strategy?

2. 'A high price needs marketing support'. Discuss.

3. A company must consider many factors when setting prices. Outline the internal and external pricing factors that should be considered before deciding the pricing strategy to be adopted.

4. Which pricing strategy should be used for each of the following products:

   -A new type of breakfast cereal?

   -A watch with a mobile phone built into it?

   -Personal computers?

Key Terms

Competitive bidding	Loss leader	Pricing
Demand	Off-peak pricing	Promotional pricing
Discounts	Penetration	Psychological pricing
Economy pricing	Premium pricing	Skimming
Geographic pricing	Price elasticity	

Chapter 10

Place

Introduction

Place is the term used in the marketing mix to mean distribution. Distribution involves all the activities necessary in getting a product to a customer. When you buy a can of Coke, it has probably been produced in a factory, transported to a wholesaler, sold on to a retailer and finally it is on the shelf and available for you to buy. All of these activities are distribution or 'place' activities. Alternatively, you may have bought a product via the internet and the product is delivered to your home or place of work. Again, the activities involved in getting the product from the seller to your home are distribution activities.

In this chapter, we shall look at distribution from two perspectives: channels of distribution and physical distribution. Channels of distribution refer to the organisations involved (distributors, wholesalers, etc) in making a product available to customers. Physical distribution refers to the physical transportation, handling and storage of products necessary to make products available to customers.

Channels of Distribution

Deciding on the channel of distribution for any product is essential as it impacts directly on all other areas of the marketing mix. Channels with several intermediaries add cost to a product. This means that the selling price may increase. The type of intermediary used will affect the way a product is promoted and advertised. So let's look at the types of channel available to an organisation. Figure 10.1 provides an overview of several typical channels of distribution along with examples of companies that use each type of channel. You should note that companies often use different types of channels simultaneously. The first channel (producer to customer) is known as a direct channel of distribution. All the others channels displayed in Figure 10.1 are indirect channels of distribution because channel intermediaries are used.

CHANNELS	EXAMPLES
Producer ➤ Customer	Barclays Bank Amazon Books John Laing Grattan
Producer ➤ Distributor/agent ➤ Customer	Ford Estate Agents Xerox JCB
Producer ➤ Retailer ➤ Customer	Heinz Nike Nestle
Producer ➤ Wholesaler ➤ Retailer ➤ Customer	Heinz Coca-cola Nestle
Producer ➤ Distributor/agent ➤ Retailer ➤ Customer	Chanel Perfume Levi Jeans

Figure 10.1 An Overview of Distribution Channels

The marketer's task is to decide on the most suitable channel of distribution for the products or services it sells. The first decision is ultimately whether to use a direct channel or not. Because of the growth in direct marketing via the internet (promoting directly to customers), the use of direct channels is on the increase.

Direct Channels of Distribution

Business-to-business companies and services companies usually use direct channels of distribution. In the case of the business-to-business marketer such as the construction company John Laing, this is essential because of the nature of the market and the nature of the product/service. Companies of this type rely on their own sales force to build relationships with customers and to make sales. (You should note that business-to-business companies also use indirect channels of distribution, particularly when selling goods internationally.)

For services, selling direct to customers is the norm. A service is actually produced and consumed simultaneously and so direct channels are essential. For a fuller discussion of services marketing you should refer to Chapter 12 of this book.

Alongside this, the use of direct channels of distribution is increasing for consumer goods companies. Many companies provide web sites where consumers can make purchases direct from the producer. Car companies have been getting a lot of press lately for their direct marketing activities. From a consumer perspective, the benefit of buying directly from the manufacturer is often related to price. Without intermediary mark-ups, the selling price is often lower.

The main benefit of a direct channel is that it allows the selling company to have direct contact with its customers. Because of this, it can gain customer knowledge and build relationships with customers. For instance, if you buy something via the internet, you often provide extensive information about yourself. You probably provide details such as your age, job and marital status (alongside credit details). This information allows a company to better understand its customer profile so that it can better satisfy their needs. By building relationships with customers, a company may gain competitive advantage.

On the other hand, a company that sells direct to its customers often becomes involved in physical distribution activities. It may have to develop expertise in an area in which it has not traditionally operated.

Indirect Channels of Distribution

This involves the use of channel intermediaries or 'middlemen'. Although cost is added to a product throughout the channel, intermediaries can play a vital role in distribution. Intermediaries perform the following functions:

Promotion: intermediaries often promote products to their customers. For instance, Tesco will provide offers such as 'two for one' on Heinz products.

Display and merchandising: intermediaries display products to their greatest advantage – thus enticing potential customers to buy. Next time you are in a retail outlet, pay attention to the way products are displayed and arranged. Often, a manufacturer may not have the expertise necessary to do this activity.

Holding inventory: stock holding costs can be high. Warehousing, security, heating and lighting are often required. Intermediaries take on some of the stock holding costs because they hold stock so that customers can buy from them.

Information: intermediaries can provide information about customers and their needs and wants. They can be in direct contact with customers and may have extensive knowledge. Intermediaries may not wish to share this information as any knowledge about customers can help to achieve competitive advantage. However, manufacturers can learn about markets through the types and quantities of products that intermediaries order from them.

Risk taking: intermediaries take on the risk of not selling products. Intermediaries usually buy products and then resell them (apart from Agents who facilitate a sale, see Chapter 13).

Physical distribution activities: intermediaries often perform the function of physically moving goods. This saves both time and cost for a manufacturer.

Breaking bulk: manufacturers frequently want to sell goods in large quantities. Therefore, intermediaries perform the function of breaking bulk. Wholesalers sell in smaller quantities to retailers and retailers, in turn, sell single items to consumers.

Convenience: Intermediaries offer convenience to customers because of their locations. In the case of consumers, if supermarkets did not exist, we would have to visit several different manufacturers in several different locations to make our purchase. Likewise in the business-to- business market. Distributors and agents often operate internationally. They provide business customers with the convenience of dealing locally when making purchases.

Choice: many intermediaries sell products from different manufacturers. From a customer perspective, product choice is often important.

Product support: intermediaries often offer support services such as services for cars.

These functions are essential. So, it is not a case of which functions should be performed, but who should perform them. In direct channels the manufacturer will perform the functions. In indirect channels, the intermediary will perform them. So, selecting suitable channels of distribution is essential. The next section of this chapter looks at distribution decisions. Selecting channels of distribution is a crucial distribution decision.

Distribution Decisions

There are three major decisions in distribution: the level of market exposure required, the selection of suitable channels of distribution and channel management techniques. We will deal with each of these areas in turn.

Market Exposure

Market exposure relates to the level of availability of a product to prospective customers. Think about it. You are more likely to see a Ford dealer than a Rolls Royce dealer in many areas. Why is this the case? Many more Ford cars are actually sold than Rolls Royce cars. The market for Ford cars is much larger. Ford offer a range of cars to suit the average family and/or business person. Therefore, Ford cars must be easily available if they are to reach their target market. On the other hand, Rolls Royce cars are quite elite. They are expensive and only a small segment of the population can afford one. Therefore they do not need to be so widely available. Generally, there are three levels of market exposure.

Intensive distribution: products that are intensively distributed are widely and easily available. They are usually products that rely on mass sales to achieve profits because the profit per item sale is low, for example FMCG's (Fast Moving Consumer Goods). Coca-cola intensively distributes its products. You can buy a can of Coke from the supermarket, local shops, bars, vending machines, etc. Intensive distribution provides customers with maximum opportunities to buy a product.

Selective distribution: in this case, products may be easily available, but in a limited number of outlets. Perfume is good example of a product that is selectively distributed. It is sold in chemists and department stores.

Exclusive distribution: if the product is elite or unique, the manufacturer may wish for an image of exclusivity to be built around it. Therefore, it will not be widely available. Again, Rolls Royce is an example of a product that is exclusively distributed. The lack of availability helps to build the product image. Additionally, each sale achieves a high level of profit and the target market is relatively small. So mass selling is unnecessary.

Channel Selection

Selecting suitable channels of distribution is a strategic decision. It directly relates to the marketing and corporate objectives of the company. It is further complicated by the fact that a company may wish to operate several different types of channel simultaneously The following factors should be considered in order to select suitable channels of distribution.

Corporate and marketing objectives: if a company wishes to pursue market share objectives, it may opt for channels that allow intensive levels of distribution. This might involve the use of indirect channels. If a company wishes to pursue profitability, it could use direct channels of distribution. However, if performing all the distribution functions itself, a company will incur additional costs.

Location of customers: if customers are geographically widely dispersed, the use of intermediaries may be vital to reach them.

Market size: again, a large market size may require the use of intermediaries to reach all potential customers. This explains the more common use of direct channels in business markets where the potential number of customers is relatively low.

Customer needs: we know that marketing is about satisfying customer needs. Therefore, channel selection should also be based on the needs of customers. Companies require information about how, when, where and why customers buy goods so that they select suitable channels.

Product attributes: a perishable good has a limited life span and so channels must be selected that allow the product to reach customers as quickly as possible. If a product is highly technically, it may require explanations during selling and after sales-servicing. A manufacturer might opt to provide these services itself, or be selective in its choice of channel to allow these services to be performed.

Competition: channels may have to be selected that allow a company's products the same level of exposure as that of competing products. Therefore, industry norms for distribution often develop. Daewoo had a large impact on the UK car market when it effectively ignored the distribution norms of the car industry. When it first entered the UK market, Daewoo sold cars directly to consumers rather than through traditional dealers. It was quite innovative in its distribution approach.

Expertise: if a company has expertise in terms of distribution it may opt to operate direct channels. If a company does not have expertise in this area it may opt for more indirect channels to benefit from the functions performed by intermediaries.

Once the type of channel(s) has been decided, the actual intermediaries (if they are being used) must be selected. For instance, a manufacturing company may wish to sell to retailers and avoid distributors and wholesalers. It must then select the retailers it will distribute through. Malcolm McDonald recommends the following criteria be considered when selecting intermediaries.

Do they now, or will they, sell to our target market segment?
Is their sales force large enough and trained well enough to achieve sales forecasts?
Is the geographical location adequate?
Are their promotional policies and budgets adequate?
Do they satisfy customer after-sales requirements?
Are their product policies consistent with our own?
Do they carry competitive lines?
What are their inventory policies?
Are they creditworthy?

So channel selection is a two stage process. Firstly, the type of channel should be selected and, secondly, the specific intermediaries (if using) should be selected. This is perhaps a rather simplistic approach. The UK retail market has evolved to such an extent that often it is the intermediary, rather than the manufacturer, that decides the goods that will be sold.

In the UK the supermarket chains are very powerful. Tesco, Sainsbury, Asda and Safeway hold so much of the FMCG market that, in many cases, they are able to dictate the products they will sell, the prices they will buy in at and the promotional activities they will perform. To be successful in the UK market, manufacturers of FMCG's often build their distribution strategy around building relationships with these vital intermediaries.

Managing Channels of Distribution

Once channels and intermediaries have been selected, a company will consider ways of managing a channel. Remember, it is the intermediary that deals with the end customer. The success and reputation of a product may depend on the intermediary. For instance, when buying electrical goods you may, to some extent, rely on the advice and service provided by the retailer. If the retailer provides bad service, you may not purchase the product. Therefore, the relationship of the manufacturer and retailer is an important one if both parties are to achieve their own objectives.

Channel management is essential. It is an important aspect of the whole concept of relationship marketing (see Chapter 14). Channels of distribution are systems that should be effective and efficient. If each channel member considers itself distinct then the channel may become ineffective because individual members may take actions that are disadvantageous to other members. This may cause conflict within the channel. Remember, each channel member is an individual business with its own objectives. Therefore, building a network or relationship throughout the channel is essential.

The manufacturer might provide support and assistance to channel members. It could do this by providing training, technical support and/or promotional support. More tangible support could be given through higher margins, special deals and cooperative advertising. It is also important that targets are established and agreed with intermediaries so that intermediaries know what is expected of them and so that their performance can be measured. Targets might include sales targets, levels of inventory held and types of services offered to the customer. To build the relationship, the manufacturer might agree targets that it will also achieve in terms of delivery times and quality of products.

Avoiding channel conflict is key to successful distribution. Conflict may arise if the targets mentioned above are not achieved or where one of the channel members is very powerful (see the supermarket example mentioned above). Vertical Marketing Systems (VMS) have developed to help alleviate channel conflict. A VMS can take three forms: corporate, administered or contractual.

A corporate VMS is where one of the channel members owns other channel members in the distribution channel. For instance, breweries in the UK are often both manufacturers and retailers. The brewery then has complete control over the products it makes, the way they are promoted and the prices they are sold at. It also offers the benefit of creating a distinct barrier to entry for competitors.

An administered VMS is achieved because one channel member is more powerful than other channel members. Again, the supermarkets in the UK are more powerful than many of their suppliers and so the supermarkets can dictate selling terms, etc. This is not a good example of relationship marketing as an administered VMS may be at the reluctance of weaker channel members.

A contractual VMS, minimises conflict through formal contractual arrangements. Perhaps the best example of this is franchising. Franchises are businesses or channel intermediaries that contractually agree to sell the goods of a franchisor. Examples of franchises are The Body Shop and Benetton. The shop owners sell and promote the goods of the franchisor under a legally binding contractual arrangement. Franchising as a means of distribution is further discussed in Chapter 13 of this book.

Physical Distribution Management

Physical distribution is concerned with the actual movement of the goods through the distribution channel. It is an area which demands a strategic approach because it is a high cost activity. Improvements in physical distribution may result in increased profits because of decreased costs. In terms of customer satisfaction, it is also important. To satisfy customers, goods must be in the right place at the right time. More and more companies are becoming concerned with physical distribution because of the increase of direct channels of distribution.

Effective physical distribution includes order processing, warehousing, inventory, materials handling and transportation. Each of these activities should be integrated and coordinated to achieve a complete distribution or logistics system.

Before any goods are physically moved, orders should be processed. Technology has helped to speed up this process. Orders can be placed by phone or by post from the customer or intermediary although the advent of electronic data interchange (EDI) has further speeded up this process. EDI means that computers can transmit order information. Take for example a retailer with EPoS (Electronic Point of Sale) terminals – you might recognise it as a till or cash register. The retailer, through the EPoS system, is able to monitor sales and identify products for reordering automatically. In many instances, the EPoS terminal actually automatically reorders goods when necessary, i.e. when stocks are low.

Electronic ordering has helped to improve the efficiency of order processing. Fewer mistakes also mean that it is a much more efficient process. From a consumer perspective, we are now able to order goods directly over the internet. We can place our order, give our credit details and the goods are delivered direct to our homes.

The next link in the physical distribution system is warehousing. Most companies store goods or hold inventory until the goods are sold. The number and location of warehouses are important if orders are to be fully satisfied.

Inventory (stock) is held at warehouses. You must remember that while stock is being held it is incurring cost. Therefore, a company will want to hold as little inventory as possible while still having the ability to satisfy customer orders. This is a vital decision area. Too much stock is costly. Too little stock may result in customer dissatisfaction. In fact, many companies now operate Just-in-Time (JIT) systems. JIT requires that littleor no inventory is held. Rather, stocks are delivered to channel members as and when they are required. Tesco operates this approach. Products are delivered to their stores and, instead of being placed in the store room, they are immediately placed on the shelves. Obviously, JIT requires effective sales forecasting and efficient ordering.

During the physical movement of goods, they must be handled in such a way that they are delivered without damage. In fact, many companies concentrate on minimising the amount of materials handling. In terms of marketing, packaging becomes an important aspect of physical distribution. We know that packaging is part of the physical product in that it may attract customers. However, packaging also performs the physical function of protecting a product. Damaged packaging and goods may result in loss of sales.

Transportation is also part of a physical distribution system. It is concerned with whether goods are transported by road, air, sea or rail. The whole distribution system is concerned with cost minimisation but, to be effective, customer satisfaction must also be considered. Road and sea are perhaps the lowest-cost forms of transportation, however they are also the slowest. When deciding on the means of transportation, a company must take into account the length of time the goods are in transit as well as the cost of the transportation. Remember, customer satisfaction is at the heart of any physical distribution system and so modes of transportation should be selected with this in mind.

Summary

Place or distribution affects all other elements of the marketing mix. There are two aspects of distribution: channel management and physical distribution.

Channels of distribution can be either direct or indirect. Direct channels involve the producer selling goods directly to its customer. Indirect channels of distribution involved the use of intermediaries in the distribution channel. A producer must decide which type of channel to use. The advantage of indirect channels is that intermediaries perform many of the distribution functions such as holding stock, promotion, risk taking and convenience. Once the types of channel have been selected, specific intermediaries should be selected.

Managing a channel of distribution is essential so that customer satisfaction can be achieved. Channel members are individual organisations with their own goals and objectives. Therefore relationship marketing is essential to ensure a coordinated effort. To minimise conflict, VMS have arisen including corporate, administered and contractual VMS.

Physical distribution is the means by which the goods physically move from the producer to the customer. Physical distribution is more complex than simply selecting the mode of transportation for products. It includes order processing, warehousing, materials handling and transportation. Physical distribution is one area where a company can achieve cost benefits. However, cost minimisation is only one aspect of physical distribution. Customer satisfaction is the other. If the goods do not reach customers in good condition and at the right time, lost sales might result.

Review Questions

1. Define distribution.
2. What is a channel of distribution?
3. List and explain three functions performed by channel intermediaries.
4. What is a direct channel of distribution and why are direct channels becoming more popular?

5. List three factors that might be considered when selecting suitable channels of distribution.

6. List three factors that might be considered when selecting channel intermediaries.

7. What is a VMS?

8. What is physical distribution?

9. What are the objectives of a physical distribution system?

10. List the components of a physical distribution system.

Discussion Questions

1. Recommend suitable distribution channels for the following products and justify your recommendations:

    -a new type of chocolate bar

    -designer clothes

    -a crane

    -a photocopier.

2. Explain why a company may opt not to use intermediaries when selling goods to its customers.

3. Identify and explain the main criteria that might be considered in selecting channels of distribution.

4. Why is channel management so important? What might a manufacturer do to attempt to manage a distribution channel effectively?

5. Identify one FMCG. What types of channels does the FMCG go through? Why is more than one type of channel used?

Key Terms

Administered VMS	Exclusive distribution	Order processing
Agent	Indirect channel	Physical distribution
Channel	Intensive distribution	Place
Contractual VMS	Intermediary	Relationship marketing
Corporate VMS	Inventory	Retailer
Direct channel	Just-in-Time	Selective distribution
Distribution	Logistics	Transportation
Distributor	Market Exposure	Vertical Marketing System (VMS)
EDI	Materials handling	
EPoS	Middlemen	Warehousing
		Wholesaler

Chapter 11
Promotion

Introduction

In this chapter we will look at promotion, the fourth element of the marketing mix. Promotion is more than just advertising. It includes almost any form of communication that a company has with its customers. Indeed, it includes communication with stakeholders, suppliers, intermediaries and the general public. The range of parties that a company promotes to are known as the target audience. For this reason, the word promotion is interchangeable with the word communication in the marketing mix.

Some people might argue that promotion is not necessary if the company understands its customers and sells goods and services that satisfy its customers. This is somewhat unrealistic. If a customer does not know that a product exists, how can he buy it? Also, we already know that there are many goods and services that satisfy the same customer need or want. Therefore, promotions also help a company to persuade customers to buy its offerings, rather than those of its competitors.

The Communication Mix

There are a multitude of methods to promote products and services. For ease, it is common to approach promotion through the use of a promotions or communication mix. Figure 11.1 depicts the elements of the communication mix. You can see from this figure that there are actually five main promotional methods.

Figure 11.1 The Communication Mix

Like the elements of the marketing mix, the elements of the communication mix are integrated and coordinated to achieve an overall objective. For instance, a car advertisement on television might entice you to visit a car dealer. Once at the dealership, you rely on the information given to you by the sales person to help you make your decision to buy. There might be a sales promotion offering a free CD player if the car is purchased. All of these promotional activities work together to encourage you to make the purchase. So the elements of the communication mix are used in combination to achieve promotional objectives. Before looking at each element of the mix in detail, we will look at the definition of each one. According to Kotler:

◆ **Advertising** is any paid form of non-personal presentation of ideas, goods or services by an identified sponsor.

◆ **Sales promotions** are any short-term incentives to encourage the purchase of a product or service.

◆ **Public relations** involve building good relations with the company's various publics by obtaining favourable publicity, building up a good corporate image and handling unfavourable rumours, stories and events.

◆ **Personal selling** is any personal presentation by the firm's sales force for the purpose of making sales and building customer relationships.

◆ **Direct marketing** involves any direct communications with carefully targeted individual customers to obtain an immediate response.

The use of the communication mix is dependent on the type of product that is being sold, the market it is being sold to, the product life cycle and on whether the company is pursuing a push or a pull strategy. Each of these will now be discussed in turn.

The Product and the Communication Mix

If a product is technological or requires explanation to prospective customers, then personal selling may be the most important element of the promotional mix. For instance, when a consumer is purchasing a car, the sales person plays a very important role. The personal selling element of the mix is then supported by the other elements of the mix.

This is similar to industrial goods. Often, in business-to-business markets, products require extensive explanation. Additionally, the sales person is involved in negotiating the terms and price of the sale. Therefore, personal selling plays a vital role in communication. The sales person's activities may be supported by advertising in trade journals and publicity.

If the product being promoted is a fast moving consumer good (FMCG), it is likely to be advertised extensively. This is because FMCGs achieve low profit margins per unit sale and so, to make a profit, a high volume of sales needs to be achieved. Advertising (particularly on TV) reaches a large number of consumers.

The Market and the Communication Mix

In business-to-business markets we have already seen that effort is often concentrated on personal selling with the other communication mix elements used to support the selling effort. The major reason for this is the characteristics associated with business markets. There are usually a fewer number of customers but each sale may be relatively high in value.

In consumer markets, most of the promotion budget may be allocated to advertising and sales promotion activities. However, more and more direct marketing activities are being used in consumer markets, mainly because of the growing use of the internet.

The PLC and the Communication Mix

The PLC is a useful tool to help with communication mix decisions. At the introduction stage, companies are likely to rely on advertising, direct marketing and public relations activities to build awareness of the product. At the growth stage advertising may still be used but this may be supported by sales promotion and/or personal selling activities.

We know that most products are most profitable during the maturity stage of the PLC. At this stage, sales promotion activities are often used and advertising is used to remind customers to continue to purchase. At decline, communication activity is often minimal and used to get rid of any remaining stocks.

This discussion of the PLC and the communication mix is a general one. The PLC is a useful tool but the other factors (the market, the product) must be considered when making mix decisions.

Push and Pull Strategies and the Communication Mix

Figure 11.2 provides an overview of push and pull strategies. When a company is pursuing a push strategy, it promotes to channel intermediaries to encourage them to stock the products. This means that when customers want to buy the product, it is readily available. Push strategies normally involve the use of sales promotion and personal selling.

When a company is pursuing a pull strategy, it promotes its products to the final customers to encourage them to buy. They are encouraged to demand the product from intermediaries. Pull strategies normally involve the use of advertising, direct marketing activities and consumer sales promotions.

In reality, companies that market products to the consumer market pursue both strategies simultaneously. In other words, when a consumer enters a store to purchase a product he has seen advertised, it is readily available because the retailer has been encouraged to stock it.

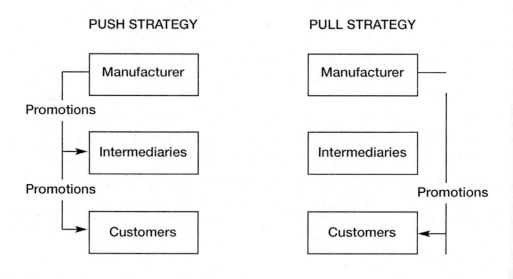

Figure 11.2 Push and Pull Strategies

Advertising

This is probably the form of promotion that you are most familiar with. We see advertisements on TV, hear them on the radio and see them in magazines. Advertising can be an expensive form of promotion. Think about the costs involved in producing a TV advertisement as well as the cost of booking into the TV scheduling. BT spends approximately £130 million a year on advertising. Dixons spends about £100 million. Because of the costs associated with it, any advertising campaign should follow a logical planning process. Figure 11.3 provides an overview of the steps involved in planning an advertising campaign. We will look at each of these steps in turn to get a better understanding of advertising. You should understand that advertising is used by both consumer marketers and business-to-business marketers. The major difference is that different budgets and media are used. For example, a consumer marketer may use TV and newspapers for advertising, while a business marketer may use trade magazines. However, the process described in Figure 11.3 is useful for both types of company.

Step 1: Identify Target Audiences

The target audience is the people or organisations that the company is advertising to. Identifying the target audience as specifically as possible is the basis of the rest of the process. Companies that have followed a thorough segmentation process should already be able to fully identify their target audience. Generally, the type of information needed includes the geographic location of the target audience, the age, income, sex and attitude of the target audience (if in consumer markets) and the levels of competition that exist in that market. The more the advertiser knows about his target audience, the more successful the campaign will be. The whole of the campaign will be targeted to this audience. Have you ever seen an advertisement and thought it was stupid? Perhaps this is because you were not part of the target audience being communicated to. On the other hand, are there specific advertisements that you enjoy and understand? Perhaps you are part of that target audience.

Step 2: Define Advertising Objectives

The objective of any advertising campaign is usually concerned with informing, persuading or reminding. Informative advertising is often used at the introduction stage of the PLC. It is used to inform potential customers that a new product exists. Persuasive advertising is used at later stages of the PLC to encourage customers to buy from a particular company, i.e. to persuade customers that they should be loyal to a brand. During the maturity phase of the PLC it is important to remind customers that the product still exists so that they continue to purchase it. Figure 11.4 overviews advertising objectives and the PLC.

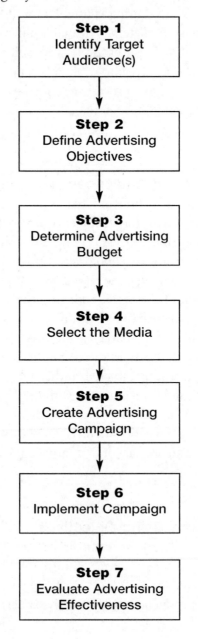

Figure 11.3 Typical Steps in Planning an Advertising Campaign

It is important that advertising objectives are SMARTER (see Chapter 2) so that the advertising effectiveness can be evaluated at the end of the campaign.   Objectives can be expressed in financial terms such as increasing sales or in more qualitative terms. For instance, if the objectives are concerned with informing customers then a company could evaluate the effectiveness of its campaign by monitoring awareness of the brand or product both before and after the campaign.

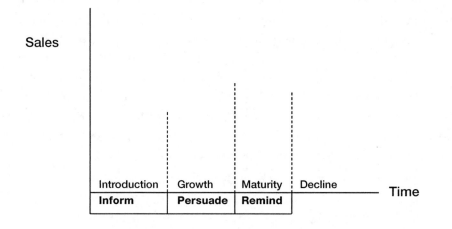

Figure 11.3 Advertising Objectives and the PLC

Step 3: Determine the Advertising Budget

Most companies actually determine the advertising budget at this stage of the process.   The amount of money made available for advertising is calculated as a percentage of sales of profits. Although this method is valid because it is simple to calculate, it could be detrimental. Think about it. If sales decrease, then advertising budget also decreases. If advertising is decreased, then the result might again be further decrease in sales.

Perhaps a more logical approach to determining the budget is the *objective and task* method. This method means that once the objectives of the campaign are determined, the tasks needed to achieve them can then be listed. The costs of the tasks are then calculated to arrive at the budget. This method is strategic in nature. It asks: what do we want to achieve and how much money do we need to achieve it? However, in practice it is rarely used.

Step 4: Select the Media

It is important to select appropriate media so that the advertising campaign can achieve its objectives. Companies can advertise on TV, radio, the internet, in magazines, newspapers, billboards and in the cinema. More and more advertising media are appearing everyday. We now see adverts on the side of buses, on taxis, on the back of tickets and even on Chinese takeaway cartons. The advantages and disadvantages of each type of media must be carefully considered before a selection is made. The media must be considered in conjunction with the target audience and the objectives of the campaign. Figure 11.5 overviews the advantages and disadvantages of some of the major advertising media available.

Once the selection of media is made, a schedule should be developed. The goal here is firstly to communicate to the largest possible number of people in the target audience with the available budget and secondly to achieve the appropriate reach and frequency for the target audience within the available budget. Reach refers to the number of people within the target audience that actually see or hear the advertisement. Frequency is the number of times these people were exposed to the advertisement. The media schedule will list the dates and timings of all the advertisements.

Because the worldwide web is a relatively new phenomenon, it is worth a special mention here. The web has offered a new advertising medium to the business world and its popularity is increasing. It is only one advertising medium available but, as customers, we tend to be rather surprised if a company does not have a web site. Therefore many companies use it because it is expected rather than because it adds anything to their promotional strategy. They have not yet discovered ways of fully exploiting the potential of the medium.

MEDIUM	ADVANTAGES	DISADVANTAGES
TV	Use of colour movement, sound; high reach, credible	Costly, limited exposure time, audience can switch over
Radio	Ability to target regional audiences, relatively inexpensive, wide selection of commercial stations	Lack of visual stimulation, limited exposure time
Newspapers	Ability to target specific audience, can provide extensive information timely, credible	Production quality often poor, reader can ignore ad, often black and white
Internet site	Relatively inexpensive internet use is increasing, can target effectively, can tie in with direct marketing activities	Audience may not have internet access, security, audience may not access site, can be difficult to register unique domain names
Magazines	Can gain international coverage, prestigious image, colour ads, long-life (if monthly), can target specialist audiences	Reader can ignore ad, can be expensive

Figure 11.5 An Overview of the Advantages of Disadvantages of Advertising Media

Step 5: Create Advertising Messages

The advertising message is concerned with the issues or points that should be made in the advertisements, i.e. the content of the advertisements. This will be based on the objectives of the campaign, the target audience, the media that has been selected and the product or service itself. Advertising messages can be strong communicators. 'Just do it' brings Nike to mind immediately. No matter how much money is spent on advertising, it will fail if the message does not gain attention or communicate with the target audience. Additionally, customers can change channels or look for new internet sites at the touch of a button. Therefore, the advertising message must be strong.

Many companies hire advertising agencies to develop their advertising messages. Staff of agencies are often creative and have an understanding of audiences. It is perhaps worthwhile paying an agency to develop the message (and the adverts) as the advertising budget may be wasted otherwise.

Stage 6: Implement the Campaign

Careful monitoring and coordination of any advertising campaign is essential. It is similar to project management. Many organisations such as production and film companies, media companies, printers, photographers and artists are involved in advertising; they all require coordination. The schedules developed at Stage 4 of this process should be adhered to.

Stage 7: Evaluate Advertising Effectiveness

Measuring the effectiveness of advertising can be a difficult and costly exercise. There are various methods for actually measuring effectiveness. Some companies pre-test (before campaign) and post-test (after campaign) their advertising. For instance, advertisements are pre-tested on customers to ascertain how they respond to the advertisement. Post-testing is done to test whether the campaign objectives have been achieved. This might be done by asking people whether they recognise an advertisement or product.

Effectiveness can also be evaluated through measuring the changes in sales. Obviously, sales levels before and after the campaign must be compared. However, this method of evaluation should be treated with caution. Many other variables affect customers' buying behaviour. A high increase in sales may not be the result of good advertising; it may be related to changes in pricing or distribution.

Sales Promotion

Sales promotions are short-term activities that encourage customers to purchase now rather than later. How many times have you been in a shop and bought something you did not need right now because it was being sold in a 'buy one, get one free' deal? This type of sales promotion activity has three main benefits for the seller. Firstly, it encourages you to buy. Secondly, it is making two unit sales rather than one. In other words, the seller has taken more market share. Thirdly, it encourages customer loyalty.

Sales promotions can be used in both push and pull strategies. In push strategies, the sales promotion is aimed at intermediaries. In pull strategies, the sales promotion is aimed at the customer or consumer. The following sales promotion activities are aimed at intermediaries:

- ◆ Cash discounts, particularly if the intermediary bulk buys.

- ◆ Credit facilities which may be attractive to smaller intermediaries.

- ◆ Competitions such as a free holiday for the intermediary that sells the most products.

- ◆ Point-of-sale material may be offer to smaller retailers. For instance, Coca-Cola provides fridges for retailers to stock its products. Haagen-Dazs provides freezers for its products.

- ◆ Training is often provided by manufacturers. Nike sends its own staff to sports retailers to train them on the benefits of Nike products.

These are only a few of the types of sales promotions activities that might be used but the discussion provides an indication of push strategy promotions. These incentives encourage intermediaries to stock the products and can be used to pursue a strategy of intensive distribution. Also, if the intermediary is happy with the 'deal' he gets, he may further push the products to his customers.

The following promotions are aimed at consumers:

- ◆ **Price-off packs:** the manufacturer prints money-off vouchers on packaging, for example '20p off'.

- ◆ **Premiums:** small gifts in packs, for example toys in cereal boxes. McDonald's often use this form of promotion. The company offers a range of children's toys with its value meals.

- ◆ **Self-liquidating premiums:** customers collect tokens on packs and send them to the supplier for free gifts, for example tokens from coffee jars for coffee mugs.

- ◆ **Sampling:** samples are often given away 'in stores to potential customers to encourage them to trial the product. Manufacturers may also send samples to consumers' homes.

- ◆ **Buy one, get one free:** a particularly popular sales promotion activity. An alternative to this approach is the buy two get the third item free.

- ◆ **In-store displays:** a good example of this is multiple product promotions when two or more complementary products are sold together. Supermarkets often do this with beer and crisps.

- ◆ **Price promotions:** this includes seasonal sales as well as discounts within the store.

- ◆ **Free gifts:** perhaps a free CD with the purchase of a stereo.

- ◆ **Loyalty cards:** this has perhaps been one of the largest growth areas in recent years. Retailers offer customers a loyalty card on which they can collect points. These points can be redeemed for money or products in-store. An example of a loyalty card is the Tesco Club Card. The added benefit of loyalty cards is that the retailer gains valuable information about its customers. A database of customers can be generated and the retailer can gain knowledge of its customer profile, buying habits and the sales promotion activities that they respond to.

The use of sales promotion continues to grow in popularity. This might be attributed to the fact that it is less expensive than advertising

Public Relations

Publicity is concerned with news stories and/or editorial comments in the press, on the radio and on TV. Like advertising, it is non-personal but, unlike advertising, it is not paid for by the company. Public relations is the attempt to manage the type of publicity that a company or a product generates. What you must remember is that publicity is essentially uncontrollable. A journalist can publish any story he wishes (constrained only by the laws of libel). A marketer has little control over the journalist. Consider the recent negative publicity that BMW received after it sold Rover. On the other hand, consider the positive publicity that Richard Branson is often able to generate. This type of coverage is read or seen by both customers and other publics of the company. Through the use of public relations activities, a marketer can attempt to influence a journalist or provide newsworthy stories.

So, although publicity is free, public relations activities can be costly. Nonetheless, PR is significantly less costly than advertising. It is also more credible. The average person will read and believe a news story while he might be suspicious of advertisements. Adcock et al state that the following areas are within the scope of public relations.

Editorial/broadcast material: this includes press conferences, news/press releases, personal interviews and press visits. Press releases are one of the most common methods of generating publicity. The marketer actually issues a story to the media in the hope that it will be published. The press release may be about the company or indeed any of its products. Because it is not paid for, there is no guarantee that a press release will be used by a journalist. In fact, most are not used. Another frequently-used publicity vehicle is the press conference. You have probably seen on television the government give a press conference when a new policy is being announced. A press conference provides a public face for a company or organisation and allows the company to have control over what is being announced. However, journalists may ask questions that are difficult to answer.

Media relations: marketers often attempt to build relationships with key journalists and editors. The benefits of this are two-fold. An editor may be more inclined to print a press release if he has a good relationship with a company or is at least familiar with it. Often, editors must fill their pages and so they may be inclined to use press releases from companies with which they are familiar. Additionally, if a journalist is about to release a negative story, he may be more inclined to call the marketer or company for comments thereby also providing forewarning that news is about to break.

Controlled communications: this includes annual reports, leaflets and magazines. If you have a BT phone line you have probably read some of the communications the company sends to you with your bill. These leaflets are designed and distributed by the company at a relatively low cost.

Face-to-face events: this type of PR activity includes conferences, exhibitions and open days and is useful for generating good will. It has the added benefit that the conference or exhibitions may be newsworthy and so generate additional publicity.

PR has several advantages over the other communication mix elements. We have already mentioned the fact that it is less costly and more credible than advertising. It also offers a company the opportunity to provide in-depth information. An advert often contains a limited amount of information because it has to be attention grabbing and communicate the main message within a relatively short space of time. A press release can discuss and describe complex issues and, because the reader perceives it to be a news story, it will be read. Also, a press release or news item will generate a larger audience than adverts – again this is perhaps because the audience is not aware that it is being targeted and so does not switch channels or turn the page.

A company might also gain publicity or media coverage through sponsorship. You have perhaps noticed that the Marlboro brand of cigarettes has been associated with Formula 1 racing. This type of publicity is beneficial for cigarette companies. They receive media coverage (you see the brand on the car) which otherwise would be prohibited; tobacco is not allowed to be advertised on TV.

Personal Selling

The role of personal selling varies according to the types of products and markets that companies are targeting. In business-to-business marketing, personal selling may be crucial whereas in consumer markets it may play quite a subtle role. Personal selling is also more significant if a manufacturer of consumer goods uses indirect channels of distribution. In this instance, the manufacturer will use its sales force to sell to the channel intermediaries.

In this chapter, we will discuss the full scope of the sales person's activities. This discussion is therefore more related to business-to-business selling than consumer marketing. You should remember that, unlike the other elements of the communication mix, personal selling is the only face-to-face communication. The other elements of the mix are non-personal. Therefore, it is very powerful. On the other hand, personal selling is very expensive.

At this point we should also note that we are not talking about the 'hard sell'. This is an approach to selling where the customer is pressured into buying a product. Yes, the sale might be achieved. However, the customer might be dissatisfied and may warn friends, family and colleagues not to buy from the company. A marketing orientated company will use selling to communicate effectively with its customers and to ensure that the products they buy directly match their needs. In this way, repeat business is more likely. It is estimated that it is five times cheaper to do business with existing customers than with new customers. Therefore, building a relationship with customers is essential. The sales force is in an excellent position to do this.

Personal selling can encompass many activities. The sales person may be responsible for the following.

- ◆ **Prospecting:** identifying prospective customers.
- ◆ **Presenting the products:** explaining the benefits of a product to prospective customers. The sales person may spend his day travelling between customers.
- ◆ **Closing the sale:** using negotiation skills.
- ◆ **Building a relationship:** the sales person may be responsible for

ensuring that the customer is satisfied with the product(s) and has no problems.

◆ **Gathering customer information:** because the sales person has face-to-face contacts he can gather knowledge about customers and their needs and wants. This may be an important source of new product ideas.

You can see that the job of the sales person is varied and therefore many skills are required. The sales person may not be based in an office. He may be travelling many miles. Because of the isolation, it is important that the sales force is wel-managed. Otherwise, the sales force may become demotivated. This may result in failure to achieve sales targets. Careful selection of sales personnel is essential, as is managing and motivating them once they have been recruited. Hill and O'Sullivan suggest that motivation and management of the sales force includes three main tasks: Strategy, Structure and Support.

Sales Force Strategy

Earlier in this book we discussed the fact that the purpose of marketing objectives was to achieve corporate objectives. The sales force strategy supports marketing objectives and therefore corporate objectives. In reality, this means that each sales person has a set of targets or objectives that he works towards. The sales person's performance can then be evaluated against these targets. Some of the most common targets include the following.

◆ **Sales targets:** these are usually expressed by value or by volume.

◆ **Call frequency:** the number of times the sales person should visit each customer.

◆ **New business:** the number of new customers the sales person should bring to the company.

◆ **Costs:** the cost per sale.

Targets can also be a useful motivational tool and, therefore, care should be taken when setting them. If a target is too high, the sales person cannot achieve it. If it is too low, it is not challenging. Furthermore, achievement of targets is often linked to remuneration. We shall look at this later.

Sales Force Structure

The most common types of sales force structure are the geographical structure, the product structure, the customer-type structure and structure by account.

The geographical structure: here, each sales person is allocated a sales region where he sells the company's products. The premise of this type of structure is that it reduces travelling time and distance between customers. However, each sales person then has to perform all the selling tasks for all the products the company sells to all the customers in his region. If the product range is diverse or very technological, this may be difficult.

The product-structured sales force: here each sales person is responsible for selling a particular product or range of products. He is then able to gain specialist knowledge of these products. This is particularly useful when the company sells technically complex products or has a very diverse range of products. The downside of this approach is that each sales person will sell to a geographically dispersed set of customers. In reality, a single customer that buys from several product ranges may be called upon by several sales people from the same company.

The customer-type structure: this means that the sales force is allocated customers according to the customer's business or products. For example, a sales person may be allocated manufacturers of consumer products while another sales person is allocated hospitals. This structure allows the sales person to become more knowledgeable about his customer's needs and wants. However, as with the product-structured sales force, customers may be geographically dispersed This means that it may be hard for a sales person to provide a good level of service cost-effectively.

Of late, many companies have moved toward structuring the sales force by account. You've probably heard the term account managers. Account managers are simply sales people that have been allocated specific customer accounts. The customer accounts are usually large and warrant special attention. In other words, this type of structure is one step further than the customer-type structure. It means that the sales person can give the larger account customers greater attention.

Sales Force Support

You can see that, no matter which structure is selected, the sales force spends a lot of time away from the office. They often operate individually and so motivation is essential. There are many methods that might be used to motivate a sales force.

Remuneration: the sales force is usually paid in one of three ways: by salary only, by salary plus some commission, by commission only. Commission only involves paying an agreed amount based on the sales person achieving his targets. It can be demotivational and encourages the sales person to pursue customers using a 'hard sell' approach. The salary-only approach means that the sales person is not rewarded for finding new business or gaining large orders. In other words, he is paid whether he sells or not. Many companies operate the salary plus commission approach. This method ensures the sales person has some secure income while he can achieve a higher level of income through beating his performance targets. The importance of setting targets was discussed earlier in this chapter.

Communication: because the sales person is isolated, regular communication from headquarters is essential. The development of mobile phones and email has made this easier. The sales person should not feel so isolated if communication is effective. This will also allow management better supervision of sales people in the field.

Organisational structure and culture: it is essential that the rest of the workforce understands the importance of the selling function. If the sales force is appreciated and recognised, it is likely to perform better.

Organisational support: in the field, the sales person often has to make promises to customers concerning such things as delivery times and dates. If the company fails to meet such promises, the customer may be dissatisfied. The sales person is on the front line and may have to deal directly with dissatisfied customers. Additionally, repeat sales may be lost.

The company should constantly strive to support the sales force activities.

Evaluation and appraisal: each sales person should be appraised regularly to determine areas of strength and weakness. This will help to improve skills as well as indicating to the sales person that he/she is a valued member of the work force.

Training: each member of a sales team should be sufficiently trained to have the ability to effectively sell the company products. The sales person may not attempt to sell any product with which he is not completely familiar. Also, sales skills training may aid the sales person to achieve his targets.

Competitions: many companies now run competitions such as 'sales person of the month' where the winner is given a substantial prize. If the sales force structure is well-organised so that each sales person has an equal chance of winning such a prize, this may be very motivational. Often, the prize is awarded at a social event where the sales people gather together. This has the added advantage of encouraging communication throughout the team.

Company car: many individuals see a car as a status symbol. Therefore, company cars should be selected that provide some status for the sales person.

Other benefits: alongside remuneration and company cars, there are many other benefits that a company may offer its sales force such as a pension scheme, social club membership, private health insurance, etc. You should note that thistype of benefit is not specific to the sales force. It can be used for the whole workforce.

We have seen that personal selling is an important activity. It can be much more expensive than the other elements of the communication mix. Therefore, the sales force must be managed well.

Direct Marketing

Direct marketing is perhaps the largest growth area of marketing. We discuss it here because it is an element of the communication mix.

However, this definition is perhaps too narrow. Although direct marketing is communication with carefully targeted individuals it is also a distribution method and, indeed, an entire marketing approach. For a discussion on direct marketing channels refer to Chapter 10 of this book. In terms of a marketing approach, many companies have achieved success through direct marketing as opposed to other forms of marketing. Daewoo initially used direct marketing as its sole approach to the UK car market. Dell computers primarily uses direct marketing in many of its markets. One recent success story has been Amazon.com. Amazon's entire marketing approach is based on direct marketing via the internet. Grattan uses catalogues to reach its target market. These companies see direct marketing as a tool for interacting with customers and establishing long-term relationships with them.

Direct marketing can be in the form of mail shots, telephone selling and catalogues. Figure 11.6 provides an overview of the types of direct marketing that exist. It is important that the defining feature of direct marketing is that it encourages a response. Therefore, TV, newspaper or magazine advertisements that include a phone number or form to complete are forms of direct marketing.

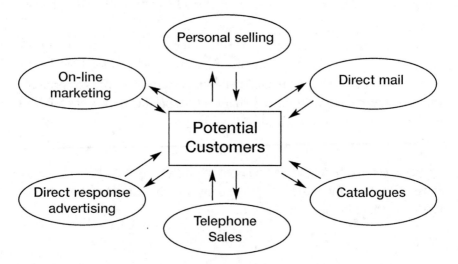

Figure 11.6 Methods of Direct Marketing

The growth in direct marketing has been supported by the growth of computer technologies such as email and the internet. Customers can order products directly from the manufacturer and, in turn, the manufacturer can encourage repeat purchases. Direct marketing via the internet offers the following advantages:

It is cost effective. It is much cheaper than printing and sending direct mail.

An internet site can contain colour and movement. This is much more stimulating to the senses than a straightforward letter.

It offers credibility to many companies.

It reaches an international audience.

Once in an internet site, the potential customer does not see other advertisements. Therefore, the internet may have more impact because it is not competing for attention.

Internet usage is increasing all the time. More and more homes have computers and most businesses now use them.

It offers customers the convenience of shopping from home.

The internet also provides a company with the means to develop a customer database. Many sites require potential customers to register. The registration 'form' might ask for details such as name, address, email address, age, job, income, etc. The company gains valuable customer information which may be used to better target customers and to keep them informed of promotions and/or new products. Customer knowledge can help a company to achieve competitive advantage. In fact, it is now possible to buy email lists. This is similar to buying mailing lists except that the list contains email addresses. The company can then email information to potential customers.

The internet can be used to build better relations with customers and to encourage them to repeat purchase. Bickerton et al provide some useful suggestions for encouraging repeat business over the internet. The seller can:

Ensure that when an order is received it takes the customer's email address. The seller can then thank them for buying and offer information on the delivery time of their goods. Amazon.com uses this tactic. Also, using the email address, the seller can send more information about products and promotions.

◆ Encourage the customer to create an account on-line. This will often encourage customers to make repeat purchases.

◆ Ensure that, once the product is delivered, it contains information about how to re-order and provides an incentive to do so.

One of the main benefits of direct marketing is that its effect can be measured more easily than other mix elements. A company can count the number of responses to a direct response advertisement. It can count the number of 'hits' on its website and it can monitor the number of replies to a mail shot. It is also relatively inexpensive and can be used to support other forms of promotion.

Summary

This chapter has detailed the elements of the communication mix: advertising, sales promotion, public relations, personal selling and direct marketing. Like the marketing mix, the elements can be used and coordinated to achieve optimum results. The way the communication mix elements are used depends on the product, the market, the PLC and whether the company is pursuing a push or pull strategy.

Advertising can be used in both business-to-business and consumer markets. However, the advertising medium used will vary according to the market. It can be expensive and so careful planning is necessary to ensure it is effective.

Sales promotion activities encourage customers to buy now rather than later. These activities can be targeted at intermediaries or at the end customer.

Publicity is generated whether a company is involved or not. Public relations is the attempt to manage the publicity that a company or product generates.

Personal selling is the only element of the communication mix that offers a company the ability to deal face-to-face with customers. It is expensive and is utilised by business-to-business marketers.

Direct marketing is growing in popularity and this growth might be attributed to increased internet usage. Direct marketing is more than just promotion. Many companies use it as their entire marketing approach.

Review Questions

1. What is the purpose of communication with customers?
2. What are the elements of the promotional mix?
3. List three advertising media and note the advantages and disadvantages of each one.
4. Explain the terms 'push strategy' and 'pull strategy'.
5. Define sales promotion.
6. List five sales promotion techniques.
7. Why is publicity more credible than advertising?
8. What is a press release?
9. Explain the ways in which a sales force might be structured.
10. List three ways to motivate a sales force.
11. Why has direct marketing become more popular in recent years?
12. List five direct marketing techniques.
13. What is database marketing?

Discussion Questions

1. Explain why more budget is allocated to sales promotion than advertising in some markets.
2. Select a company with which you are familiar. Identify the public relations activities it has led in the last year.
3. Suggest methods an organisation might use to evaluate the effectiveness of an advertising campaign.

4. What are the major steps involved in developing an advertising campaign?

5. Who are an organisation's publics? How can PR be used to communicate with these publics?

6. Identify three advertisements. Build a profile of the customers that you think these advertisements are targeting.

Key Terms

Account manager	Database marketing	Press release
Advertising	Direct marketing	Product structure
Advertising media	Direct-response advertising	Public relations
Advertising message	Frequency	Publicity
Audience	Geographical structure	Publics
Buy one get one free	Hard sell	Pull strategy
Catalogue	Internet	Push strategy
Communication mix	Mail shot	Reach
Customer type structure	Personal selling	Sales promotions
		Sponsorship

Chapter 12

The Extended Marketing Mix: Services Marketing

Introduction

Throughout this book we have referred to the marketing mix as the 4Ps. In this chapter, we introduce a new concept: the 7Ps. In services marketing it is necessary to use an extended marketing mix with seven instead of four elements. This is mainly because services marketing has distinct characteristics associated with it. Figure 12.1 displays the extended marketing mix. You can see that the 'additional' 3Ps are people, process and physical evidence. Each of these elements will be explained later in this chapter.

Figure 12.1 The Extended Marketing Mix

The Characteristics of Services

We have already mentioned the fact that services marketing is different from product marketing because services have distinct characteristics. These characteristics are:

Intangibility: services are not physical products. You can't smell, touch or see a service before you actually buy it. Think about the AA. This company offers a call-out service if your car has engine trouble. Members pay an annual fee for this service. However, the service does not actually exist until a mechanic is attending a car. In other words, a customer cannot see any tangible attributes of the service. For the marketer, this creates the problem of explaining a service to a potential customer. Customers need evidence that the service being sold will, when they buy it, satisfy their needs. In product marketing, the customer can see and feel a product before buying it. This is not possible in services marketing. Therefore, to make a judgement about a service a customer will look at the price, the promotional material, the location and the staff that provide the service.

Inseparability: this relates to fact that services are produced and consumed at the same time. For example, if a manufacturer has a contract with a company to service its machinery, this service only exists when it is being performed. Production and consumption of the service are inseparable, i.e. they are simultaneous. Often, customers are directly involved in the service. When you visit a hairdresser, you are involved in the production of the service. This poses problems for a marketer because the standard of service provided may be inconsistent.

Perishability: a service cannot be stored. Remember, it is intangible. It only really exists when the provider is performing the service and when the customer is involved. Production and consumption are inseparable. This poses the problem of matching supply and demand, i.e. making the service available when the customer wants it. Added to this is the fact that demand is unlikely to be steady. There may be busy periods and quiet periods. The product marketer has less problems in this area because products can be stored.

Heterogeneity: most services are labour intensive. The quality of a service often depends on the person actually performing the service. Because quality relies on people, it may be inconsistent. Think about it. A hairdresser will not be able to provide the same level of service to every customer. He will be cutting different types of hair, in different styles and his mood may change over the course of a day or a week. The service provided cannot be standardised. This is a problem that is not really faced by product marketers. It is often obvious when a product is damaged or below standard. The marketer is unlikely to sell the product in this condition.

The characteristics of services raise many issues for marketers. It is because of these characteristics that the extended marketing mix was developed.

The Extended Marketing Mix: People

'People' refers to the staff that actually provide the service. We already know that services are inseparable and heterogeneic. This is because of the high involvement of staff (people). It is interesting to note that many product marketers now recognise the importance of people when selling their products. Therefore, the people element of services marketing can apply to product marketing. If you went to a restaurant where the food was excellent but the service was poor, you may not frequent that restaurant again. Often, the quality of the service provided is dependant on the people providing it.

Selection, motivation and training are therefore paramount to the success of a service. Selection procedures should ensure that the correct person is selected for a job. It is not within the scope of this book to discuss selection procedures. Any good HRM book will overview this area.

Once selected, staff must be trained. Of course, one aspect of training is to ensure that they can perform the service. In other words a mechanic should be able to fix cars. A hairdresser should be able to cut hair. These skills are vital. However, on their own, they are insufficient. Remember, staff are interacting directly with customers. They may be building relationships with customers. Therefore, their social skills are important.

Customer service training is important. In a marketing-orientated company, all staff should recognise the importance of customer satisfaction.

As well as effective selection and training, motivation is a key aspect of the people element of the marketing mix. A person that is demotivated is likely to under perform. The result of this, in services marketing, is customer dissatisfaction. Internal marketing programmes are essential. Internal marketing is concerned with training and motivating staff. Motivated staff may be the key to customer satisfaction. Methods of motivating people include:

◆ **Internal communications:** communication between management and staff is essential for staff to be motivated. This can be in the form of company newsletters or, on a more official basis, through meetings and appraisals.

◆ **Profit share:** giving employees a share of company profits can be motivational. The employee's performance is therefore directly linked to the amount of money he receives.

◆ **Empowerment:** to a certain extent, staff should be given some discretion over the service they deliver. They should be able to adapt to customer needs rather than follow a prescribed process. This recommendation is contrary to the beliefs of many companies. If you visit McDonald's you often receive the same greeting and are asked the same questions by staff. How do you feel about this?

◆ **Recognition:** staff should be rewarded and recognised for their efforts. This can be formal (see profit share above) or informal; a simple 'thank you' or 'well done' can be motivational.

◆ **Responsibility:** providing employees with some responsibility may encourage them to care about the job more.

◆ **Promotion opportunities:** the opportunity for career advancement can be motivating.

Individuals are different. Each member of staff may be motivated by different things. It is the task of the manager to identify what motivates staff to ensure that they serve customers with enthusiasm.

The Extended Marketing Mix: Physical Evidence

Because services are intangible, it is difficult for potential customers to judge whether the service will satisfy their needs. Customers require evidence that the service is what they want. The physical evidence element of the extended marketing mix is the means by which service providers offer reassurance to their customers.

Service marketers provide brochures and internet sites so that customers can get a feel for the service before they participate in it. Premises are often well-decorated and coordinated so that customers build an image of the company. Staff are usually well-groomed and often wearing uniforms to reinforce the image of the company to the customer.

Barclays Bank for example, provides literature on all of it's available services. This literature is usually produced in the turquoise colour associated with the Barclays brand. The banks themselves are well-decorated and maintained, often with turquoise built into the colour scheme. Staff wear uniforms so that they stand out to customers and, again, turquoise is in the uniform. All of these factors provide physical evidence to customers of the standard of service they can expect from the bank.

Product marketers do not always have to consider physical evidence. The products are tangible and customers can touch, feel and perhaps sample them before they buy.

The Extended Marketing Mix: Process

The process element of services is concerned with the process or procedure that a customer follows when he interacts with the service provider. For instance, when booking a hotel the customer may call the hotel, book a room, receive confirmation by mail, stay in the hotel and check out. This is all part of the process.

Processes must be as effective and efficient as possible. Customers can become dissatisfied if they are not treated well. A lengthy queue may encourage a customer to seek the services of a competitor.

The trend to improve the process that a customer follows has been for service providers to become more automated. It is quite common, when calling a company, to be held in an automated queuing system. The purpose of such automation is to minimise the levels of variation in the service so that all customers receive standard treatment. It also decreases the levels of staff involvement. Unfortunately, many customers do not like such automated services.

The internet has offered many service providers the scope to improve their services. It is now possible to book hotel rooms, flights and even dinner reservations over the internet. This offers the customer more control because he is part of the process.

Alongside this is the fact that services are perishable; they cannot be stored. This means that a service provider must ensure that services are available when the customer wants them. In other words, a service provider must ensure that supply meets demand. Several methods are used to do this:

Encourage off-peak demand: many companies experience different levels of demand depending on the time of day, the day of the week or the month of the year. For instance, hotels are often busier during the week than at weekends. Service providers may attempt to encourage customers to buy during 'quieter' periods. A hotel will offer cut price rooms or free meals to customers who use their services at weekends.

Queuing systems: it is common to see queues a peak times in banks, post offices and shops. Customers are often not happy to queue and, so, service providers have attempted to improve their processes. Banks (as well as other companies) now encourage customers to form one queue. When a window is free, the person at the front of the queue is served. This is different from previous systems where several queues were formed at each window. Customers in this type of system often felt unfairly treated.

Staff availability: to cope with the increased levels of demand at peak time, service providers will ensure they have as many members of staff as possible. Many employees are hired for 'peak-time only' hours to ensure that demand is met.

Appointments: the use of appointments allows a service provider to ensure that it can deal with levels of demand. Through the use of appointments the provider knows how many customers will be using the service. It is common for restaurants, hairdressers and solicitors to implement appointment systems.

Summary

This chapter has highlighted the characteristics associated with services marketing: intangibility, perishability, heterogeneity and inseparability. It is these characteristics that make the marketing of services more complex than the marketing or products.

To deal with services, the marketer uses the extended marketing mix: people, physical evidence and process.

'People' is concerned with staff. Because services are labour intensive, customer satisfaction can be attributed to staff. In fact, the people element of the extended marketing mix is becoming more important to product marketers too. Staff should be selected carefully and trained and motivated to perform well.

Physical evidence involves those elements that make a service more tangible to customers. It includes location, décor, furnishings, leaflets, brochures, etc.

When buying a service a customer follows a process. It is the job of the service marketer to ensure that the process a customer follows is effective and efficient.

Review Questions

1. How does services marketing differ from product marketing?
2. List the four characteristics directly associated with services marketing.
3. What is the purpose of the extended marketing mix?
4. Explain three methods that might be used to motivate staff.
5. What is internal marketing?
6. Why is it difficult for services marketers to match supply and demand?
7. Explain the process a customer follows when booking a holiday.
8. List five ways to provide physical evidence to customer in services marketing.

Discussion Questions

1. 'The secret of services marketing is people'. Discuss.
2. Select a service provider of your choice. Identify how the company uses the extended marketing mix to satisfy its customers.
3. Explain how the Ansoff matrix (discussed in Chapter 2) might be used by a service marketer.
4. 'Staff should be treated as customers'. Discuss.

Key Terms

Extended marketing mix	Internal marketing	Perishability
Heterogeneity	Motivation	Physical evidence
Inseparability	People	Process
Intangibility		Service

Chapter 13
International Marketing

Introduction

Many organisations now operate internationally. They sell products and services in countries all over the world. Many of the companies and brands that you recognise are also recognised internationally. Nike, Coca-Cola, Nestlé, GE and Microsoft are a few examples of companies that have an international presence. The trend to sell goods internationally is growing.

In this chapter we will look at the complexities of international marketing. Essentially, marketing internationally is similar to marketing domestically. However, there are added considerations.

International Marketing Strategy

Figure 13.1 overviews the process that an organisation might follow when moving from domestic to international marketing. In this chapter, we will look at each stage of the process in detail. Although many organisations follow a process similar to this one, it does not apply to all organisations. Some companies get into international marketing by chance. For instance, the increase in direct marketing via the internet has helped many companies to sell internationally without a formalised process.

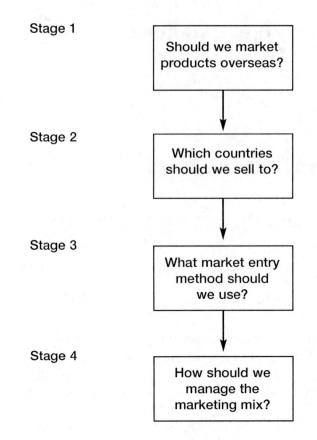

Figure 13.1 International Marketing Strategy

Stage 1: Should We Market Products Overseas?

The decision to sell goods internationally can be a difficult one. A company may have to allocate significant budget and time to ensure that an international operation is successful. Additionally, if the company has little prior experience of international marketing, the venture can involve risk.

There are many reasons why companies sell goods internationally:

◆ There is demand from customers in other countries. This offers a company the chance to increase profits.

Competition may be so intense domestically that a company is forced to seek new markets for its products.

Strategically, a company may look to international markets as a marketing development strategy (see Ansoff matrix in Chapter 2).

New markets offer a company a means to extend the product life cycle.

International markets offer a company the chance to build a global brand and gain global recognition.

It allows a company to spread risk. If sales decline in one country, the company may still be able to generate profits in other countries.

If offers a company the chance to get rid of excess capacity.

Governments often offer incentives to companies to trade internationally.

This last point is very important. When a company sells goods internationally, it is generating money – not only for itself but for the country. Generally, a government will want to export more products than it imports because this achieves a positive balance of payments. In other words, more money is coming into a country than leaving it. This is one indication of a country's wealth. A high level of exports means that the domestic market is healthy.

As well as the benefits to a company, the macro environment is developing in such a way that international trade is encouraged. Keegan summarises the forces that contribute to the growth in international trade:

Market needs: it is now recognised that, although different cultures and needs exist around the world, many consumers display similar tastes, needs and wants. This is perhaps the reason why companies like McDonald's are successful. McDonald's satisfies the same need internationally; the need for fast food. Global demand exists for many products such as industrial products, technological products, soft drinks, etc.

Technology: consumers around the world want the same products because they have seen or heard of them. Technology has aided this knowledge. The internet, television and radio have introduced products and brands to consumers internationally. Consumers now travel regularly. This allows them to see the products and services that are being sold in other countries. This knowledge means that many consumers display similar tastes, needs and wants.

◆ **Cost:** selling internationally allows companies to recover the costs of research and new product development.

◆ **Quality:** because of the increased revenue generated through international sales, companies can invest more in product design and manufacture. This leads to better quality products.

◆ **Communications and transportation:** the information revolution contributes towards the emergence of global markets. Consumers all over the world want the latest and most modern model of a product.

◆ **Leverage:** selling goods internationally allows a company to gain money and power. It benefits from economies of scale, spreads its risk and gains international recognition.

You can see that selling internationally offers a company many benefits. So, having decided that it is advantageous, a company can begin to select the countries or markets that it will enter.

Stage 2: Which Countries Shall We Sell To?

For a company that is entering international markets for the first time, the decision on which country or countries to enter is a crucial one. The same market analysis and research is required as in domestic marketing. But, the costs and time required to research international markets will be much higher. Therefore, it is essential to approach this decision methodically. Figure 13.2 suggests a process that might be followed when selecting foreign markets. It can be viewed as a screening process because countries without potential are eliminated at each stage.

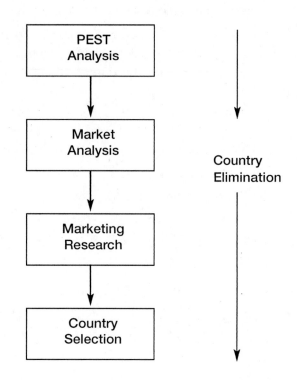

Figure 13.2 The International Screening Process

PEST Analysis

Perhaps the greatest difference between domestic and international markets is the PEST factors. Companies that are considering international markets must consider differing political, economic, social and technological factors for the first time.

Political/Legal Factors

Politically, a company should consider the role of the government and the political stability of a country. A country may become less attractive if it is politically unstable. In business terms, a country that is volatile may result in lost profits for a company.

Another consideration is that of trading blocs. Trading blocs are formed of countries that have agreed to reduce protectionist measures. For instance, the UK is part of the European Union (EU) trading bloc. The EU has 15 member nations. They are:

Austria

Belgium

Denmark

Finland

France

Germany

Greece

Ireland

Italy

Luxembourg

Netherlands

Portugal

Spain

Sweden

UK.

These countries have agreed to trade with each other without imposing protectionist measures. Protectionist measures are any actions taken by a country or government to protect the domestic market against imports.

We said earlier that governments encourage exporting to generate money. While doing this, it is usual to attempt to discourage imports. Remember, imports mean that money is leaving a country and also that companies in the domestic market face increased competition. If customers buy the 'foreign' goods, then domestic companies lose sales and therefore profits. Governments attempt to protect their domestic industries in two ways:

Tariffs: a tariff is a tax on products entering a country. Tariffs are charged on the value of the goods or on the weight or volume of the goods. Because of these added costs, the end selling price of a product will perhaps be higher than domestically produced products.

Non-tariffs: non-tariff barriers are less obvious than tariff barriers but they do add cost to a product. Non-tariff barriers include:

Quotas: a limit on the amount of goods entering a country. This may be a limit on specific products or a limit on goods coming from a specific country.

Government subsidies: a government may support its domestic industries by giving subsidies to them. A company that receives a subsidy may be able to sell its goods at relatively low prices. Therefore, an international company will find it more difficult to compete.

Customs and entry procedures: administrative procedures at ports may be complex. This means that products may be held at a port for an indeterminate amount of time. It is not always possible to predict when the goods will reach the market place. This of course increases cost but also protects domestic companies because their goods will be in mass circulation.

Exchange controls: in countries such as Russia, currency is a key issue. The Russian Rouble is almost worthless internationally because it is not a hard currency. Roubles taken out of Russia cannot be converted into other currencies. Therefore, it is important for a government to build up stocks of hard currencies such as dollars. The government maintains its stock of hard currency by minimising imports; in this way, money is not leaving the country.

Legal ownership: in many countries, there are laws stipulating that any foreign company wishing to do business there must form a partnership with a domestic company. In this way, investment is ensured in the host country and a percentage of profits remains in the country.

For a British company that is considering international marketing for the first time, it might be advisable to consider only those countries within the EU initially. This may negate the need to consider protectionist measures.

Countries also operate different legal systems. For any company wishing to enter international markets, it is critical that the legal system is investigated. We already know that in some countries it is illegal to own your own subsidiary completely. Factors such as pricing regulations and promotional restrictions should be investigated.

Economic Factors

The state of the economy will be different in every country. Economic factors affect levels of demand and the ability for potential customers to actually pay for goods. At this stage of the process (see Figure 13.1), it is essential to consider economic factors such as Gross Domestic Product (GDP) per capita, living standards, energy availability and education levels.

Fortunately, such information is widely available and, often, a quick search on the internet will generate the required statistics. Companies must consider these factors in relation to the products they intend to sell.

Social/Demographic Factors

Demographics refers to the population. Knowledge of the population size and population trends is essential in order to determine whether a country is attractive or not. As with economic statistics, demographic information can be gathered quite easily.

It is also important to understand the population distribution. For instance, China might seem like a very attractive country. It is highly populated but it is also geographically immense. However, a large proportion of the population is based in Shanghai and Beijing. Therefore, a company considering the Chinese market may only consider distributing goods in city areas rather than throughout the entire country.

The culture of each country is also important. Culture is a complex set of norms, attitudes and beliefs. Figure 13.3 provides an overview of the components of culture. Each of these components may be different in every country. Culture directly affects the marketing mix and is a crucial factor in the success of a company and its products overseas.

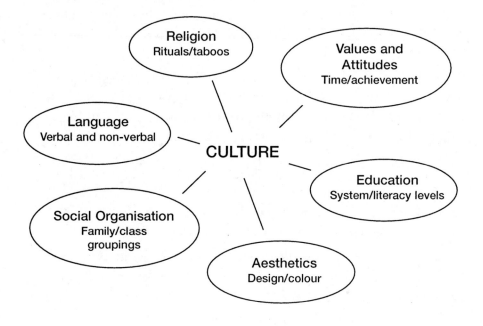

Figure 13.3 The Dimensions of Culture

Language has a direct impact on the international marketer. There are the obvious translation difficulties but the marketer should also consider non-verbal language. This is especially important if personal selling is a key promotional tool. The sales team may have to be trained in not only the local dialect but also body language and its meaning. For instance, a sales person doing business with an Arab in Saudi Arabia must be very aware of his sitting position. If the sales person inadvertently turns up the sole of his shoe, perhaps while cross his legs, the Arab will be gravely insulted. In terms of the written word, there are numerous examples of brands that, when translated, have a completely different meaning. For instance, in Italy, a campaign for Schweppes Tonic Water translated the name into Schweppes Toilet Water. Even the largest international companies have made mistakes. The name Coca-Cola in China was first rendered as Ke-kou-ke-la. Unfortunately, the Coke company did not discover until after thousands of signs had been printed that the phrase means 'bite the wax tadpole' or 'female horse stuffed with wax' depending on the dialect. Coke than researched 40,000 Chinese characters and found a close phonetic equivalent – 'Ko-kou-ko-le', which can be loosely translated as 'happiness in the mouth'.

Religion plays a key role in society in many countries. It might influence buying behaviour, social behaviour, manner of dress and ways of doing business. In the UK, we celebrate Christmas and Easter; both religious holidays that offer the marketer tremendous sales opportunities. When considering selling products internationally for the first time, it is essential that a company understands the role of religion in a society, as well as the rituals and taboos associated with it. For instance, it is very difficult to perform research on women in Arab countries because of their role in that society, even though women may be key consumers.

Values and attitudes are also different throughout the world. According to Hall (1976) countries exhibit either a 'monochronic' or 'polychronic' culture. In the UK, we have a monochronic notion of time. We dislike queuing and are keen to keep appointments. Other countries, such as France, India and Japan, have a polychronic perception. In this case, time is less of an issue. Queuing is acceptable and keeping to appointment times is not fundamentally important. It is the relationship between people that is key in these societies. When selling goods in polychronic countries for the first time, the British company can expect to hold several meetings before the subject of business is actually discussed.

Education levels also vary throughout the world. The marketer may find it difficult to package and promote his products to countries that have lower education levels.

Aesthetics, in this context, is concerned with the design and appearance of objects. In Japan, cosmetic products are often given elaborate packaging (much more so than in the UK) because the packaging is key in buying decisions.

Social organisation relates to the role of the family, the role of men and women and social class. Social classes tend to have different consumption patterns and different systems of social class exist around the world. India, for example, operates under the Caste system. Each Caste has a different standing in that society from the lower to the higher Castes. In many societies, the extended family (consisting of brother, sisters, cousins, uncles, aunts, grandparents, etc) still exists and there may be a strong emphasis on family loyalties. In fact, the family may be the main focus of buying activity.

Cultures throughout the world are wide and varied. Culture may have a strong impact on marketing mix decisions and, so, the decision on whether a country is attractive to a company may be based on the extent of cultural differences. We will return to our discussion of culture later in the chapter. At this stage of the screening process it is necessary to have a basic understanding of culture so that counties without potential might be eliminated. During the market analysis and market research stages, a more in-depth understanding of cultural issues may be required.

Technological Factors

Technology is now a part of our everyday life. You probably use a computer almost every day. When you go to the supermarket, the EPOS terminals read bar codes. You may have ordered products over the internet. We are a technologically advanced nation. This is not the case in many parts of the world.

The level of technological development may affect:

◆ The provision of support services for a product: many products require servicing and spare parts. These may not be available in less developed nations.

◆ The existence of an appropriate distribution network: TV's and computers require electricity. The internet requires a telecommunications network. These facilities may not exist.

◆ Communication with customers: advertising media may be unavailable in many countries.

These are important factors when a company is considering international markets for the first time.

Market Analysis

Having performed the first stage of the screening process, a company will now be in a position to gather more detail about countries that appear attractive to it. Remember, the purpose of market analysis is to gather further information so that countries without potential may be eliminated so that financial losses might be minimised.

The information required to analyse a market depends on the type of company and the type of products being sold. However, the following factors might be considered:

◆ **Level of existing and potential competition:** Porters Five Forces model (see Chapter 3) might be used to assess the nature of the competition within a market. This is vital. A country may appear to be attractive but there may be high barriers to entry because of existing competition.

◆ **Accessibility:** more in-depth analysis of tariffs, non-tariffs, government regulations, etc., is required at this stage. The company must assess whether the market is relatively straightforward to enter. For instance, China is often viewed as an attractive market because it offers huge market potential. However, the are many barriers to trade which make it difficult to sell goods in that country. You should note that a company may still consider entering the Chinese market because of its long-term potential.

◆ **Market size:** the potential market size must be assessed to ensure that future investment is worthwhile.

◆ **Profitability:** the investment required to move from domestic marketing to international marketing can be vast. A company must consider all the macro factors and, having taken them into account, ensure that profits can still be achieved.

At this stage of the planning process, it is also advisable for a company to consider its own capabilities. Does it have the financial resources to support an international strategy? Does it have the expertise? Does it have the production capability to satisfy increased levels of demand? The next stage of screening is marketing research. This is a costly activity domestically, but even more expensive internationally. A company should understand its own operations and longer term strategy before investing in full marketing research.

International Marketing Research

The approach to international research is, on the whole, similar to that of domestic research. The main difference is that international research is more complex and more expensive. Complexity arises from the fact that the marketer is dealing with different countries and cultures. The expense arises because the countries may be geographically widespread and research may be performed in more than one country. Therefore, before a full market research project is undertaken, the marketer should gather as much information as possible (see above).

In order to scan markets, the marketer has probably already used many secondary sources of information. For more in-depth research, further secondary research is necessary. There are a wealth of sources of international secondary information including the OECD Monthly Statistics of Foreign Trade, the World Bank Stars statistics and the IMF Direction of Trade Statistics. These sources are relatively inexpensive and quite easy to get hold of.

Much secondary information can also be gathered over the internet. Doole et al identify the following major on-line data bases:

> **Datastream:** international company and financial data and economic analysis of developed countries.

> **Text line:** a Reuters' information service on companies, industries and economics.

> **Predicast:** worldwide business and industry information.

> **Key notes:** market analysis reports.

> **SICE:** US import-export information.

> **Harvest:** international data.

The main advantage of these on-line data bases is that they are continually updated, easy to access and inexpensive. The marketer may have to pay a fee to access the information but this is nothing in comparison to gathering the information through primary research.

As with any marketing research, secondary research should always be performed first. However, there are dangers with secondary research especially internationally.

Secondary research may not be available regarding certain countries. Countries that are less developed may not actually produce economic information. Additionally, some governments may actually manipulate data so that their country appears more economically sound (and therefore attractive) than it actually is. The source of any secondary information should be checked and confirmed.

Primary research can be a lengthy process and, for a company entering international markets for the first time, it is perhaps advisable to use the services of a market research agency. Agencies offer expertise in their fields and the end cost may be lower if agency services are employed. However, for the marketer who wishes to perform the research the following factors must be considered:

◆ **Sampling may be difficult:** to derive a sample, a population is necessary. Because of the difficulties in gaining accurate secondary information, this information may not be available. Therefore, it will be difficult to actually identify a valid sample (see Chapter 4).

◆ **Some cultures may be suspicious of research:** we are accustomed to marketing research and the use of questionnaires. It is not so prevalent in many societies. Therefore, response rates may be low and the information gathered may be unreliable. In the Middle East it may be difficult to include women in research.

◆ **Questionnaires may require translation:** straightforward translation is insufficient. The translation may not illicit the desired information. Likewise, if personal interviewers are used they must speak the language and have an understanding of the culture.

◆ **If literacy levels are low**, postal questionnaires cannot be used.

◆ **A country's infrastructure** might impact on the type of research performed. Poor roads or transport networks may make personal interviewing impossible. Lack of effective telecommunications networks may make telephone interviewing impossible. An effective postal system is necessary for mailed questionnaires.

It is because of the above problems that the services of a market research agency may be employed. However, extensive research is recommended so that a country may be selected.

Stage 3: What Market Entry Method Shall We Use?

Once a country has been selected, the marketer must consider how to enter that market. In other words, which methods will be used to actually make goods available to customers overseas. Here, we are concerned with the channels of distribution that can be used. There are three major options: indirect exporting, direct exporting and direct investment. Figure 13.4 provides an overview of these three main methods of entry to overseas markets. We will discuss each method in turn. For ease, we will discuss international market entry methods from a manufacturer's view point.

Indirect Exporting

You can see from Figure 13.4 that in indirect exporting products are sold by a manufacturer to an intermediary in the UK. It is the intermediary who actually sells the products overseas. The manufacturer in this instance has very little international involvement. In terms of time and financial investment, this lack of involvement is beneficial. However, it does mean that the manufacturer has little control over the way products are sold overseas, the price they are sold at and the methods of promotion used.

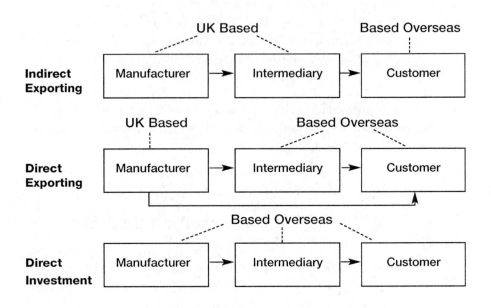

Figure 13.4 Foreign Market Entry Methods

Additionally, the manufacturer will not acquire knowledge about international markets or the customers in those markets. There are three main methods of indirect exporting. Figure 13.5 provides an overview of these methods.

Export houses: an export house is an intermediary, based in the domestic market, that acts almost as an export department. The export house will take orders from overseas customers and will buy from domestic manufacturers to satisfy these orders. In other words, it is like a wholesaler that sells goods internationally.

Buying offices: these are the buying offices of multinational corporations that wish to have a presence in the markets from which they buy. Macy's, the famous American department store, has buying offices in over 30 countries. Staff of the buying offices approach manufacturers, buy their goods and export them around the world.

Piggybacking: this is a different approach to indirect exporting. In this case, the manufacturer achieves international distribution through using the distribution network of an already established international company. The manufacturer that is new to international marketing will usually sell its products as an 'add-on' to products from the more established company. For instance, a British company that manufactures camera films may piggyback a recognised camera manufacturer that sells its products globally. The British company achieves worldwide distribution. The camera manufacturer is able to provide added value to its customers by providing films when a camera is purchased.

You can see that indirect exporting is a relatively quick entry method with a limited amount of financial investment. It also means that the domestic manufacturer does not have to consider tariff and non-tariff barriers or the increased costs of international physical distribution. However, control is in the intermediaries' hands. In addition to this, the manufacturer is gaining very little knowledge of international marketing and, therefore, long-term strategic planning is difficult.

Direct Exporting

You can see from Figure 13.4 that there are two general approaches to direct exporting. Firstly, a manufacturer may opt to sell direct to its customers with no channel intermediaries. The customers are based overseas. International direct marketing has grown in popularity because of the growth in popularity of the internet. It is also widely used by business-to-business marketers. For a fuller discussion of direct marketing you should refer to Chapters 10 and 11 of this book. The second approach is concerned with using intermediaries that are based overseas.

Direct exporting therefore involves some international activity by the domestic manufacturer. It is now involved overseas with either the end customer or an international intermediary. So, it is more of a commitment, in both time and financial terms, than indirect exporting.

Apart from direct marketing, there are four main methods of direct exporting. Figure 13.5 provides an overview of these methods.

Agents: an agent is an intermediary, based overseas, who acts on behalf of the domestic manufacturer. The agent finds customers/sales for the manufacturer and is paid on a commission basis. This type of company is rather like an estate agent. An estate agent acts on behalf of the person selling his home and receives a commission on the selling price. Because an agent is paid on a commission basis, he is motivated to sell the products. However, an agent will act for several manufacturers and careful selection of agents is essential. Internationally, agents are valuable intermediaries because they have international market knowledge and often have an established network of customers.

Distributors: the major difference between an agent and a distributor is that a distributor actually buys then resells products. A distributor based overseas may represent a manufacturer in all sales and servicing in a predetermined geographical area. Because distributors actually buy the products the domestic manufacturer takes little financial risk. However, a distributor has more control than an agent over the way products are sold and priced.

Franchising: in this case, the intermediary (the franchisee) agrees to sell products in a certain way. Franchising is usually associated with retailing rather than manufacturing. The Body Shop, McDonald's and KFC are examples of companies that have selected franchising as a means of international market entry. The company or franchiser decides the selling price of products, the store layout and other operational issues. The franchisee implements these decisions – and is contractually obliged to do so. Usually, the franchisee pays the franchiser for the right to use its name and marketing. Therefore, this is a relatively low-cost international entry method for the franchiser. However, control and management of international franchisees can be difficult.

Licensing: this is similar to franchising except that is generally involves manufacturing. In this case the licensor gives the rights to a licensee to use brand names, trademarks or processes. Perhaps this is better explained by way of an example. Disney characters are often licensed throughout the world. Disney permits licensees to use characters such as Mickey Mouse on their products. Hence, an Italian manufacturer of children's clothes may seek a licence from Disney to reproduce Mickey Mouse and print him onto clothing. Disney achieves international distribution of the Mickey Mouse character and receives payment for this. Coca-Cola provide licences to manufacturers around the world to produce the soft drink.

Direct exporting requires a higher level of involvement from the domestic company. This is advantageous in that the manufacturer is gaining international knowledge and has some control over international intermediaries and therefore sales. Although international knowledge is gained, the manufacturer still benefits from the local knowledge of the intermediaries used. On the downside, it can be difficult to find and manage suitable intermediaries and, because intermediaries are international, the manufacturer cannot be sure they are fulfilling their obligations (even if they are contractually obliged to do so).

Direct Investment

This entry method involves the greatest amount of time and financial investment and therefore is perhaps the riskiest. Figure 13.4 indicates that, in this case, the manufacturer also bases itself overseas. There are three main methods of direct investment. Figure 13.5 provides an overview of these methods.

Wholly-owned subsidiaries: this involves a manufacturer finding and acquiring a site, hiring staff and running a plant. It is a significant long-term investment. Nissan has used this approach in the UK. The Nissan factory here assembles car components but is wholly-owned by Nissan. The benefit of this approach is that the manufacturer can establish its subsidiary where low-cost labour exists. Also, it will hire local staff and so may generate goodwill. Governments are keen to encourage direct investment and will often offer subsidies to international companies.

Acquisition: rather than finding and establishing a site from scratch, many manufacturers (and other types of companies) acquire existing companies. Marks and Spencer used acquisition to enter the American market. In this case, the manufacturer acquires sites, staff and established customers – it is therefore beneficial. However, it is difficult to find a company that is suitable for acquisition.

Joint ventures: many manufacturers opt to establish a partnership, with a local partner, in the overseas country. The local partner can provide valuable local market knowledge to a manufacturer. In many countries foreign ownership is restricted and therefore, forming a joint venture is the only option.

Direct investment is a long-term approach. It could be several years before the financial outlay is recovered from direct investment activities. It is therefore a risky strategy. However, direct investment provides a manufacturer with high levels of control. It can also be used strategically to access further international markets. For instance, if a manufacturer sets up a wholly-owned subsidiary in England, it can export its goods throughout the rest of the EU without facing tariff barriers.

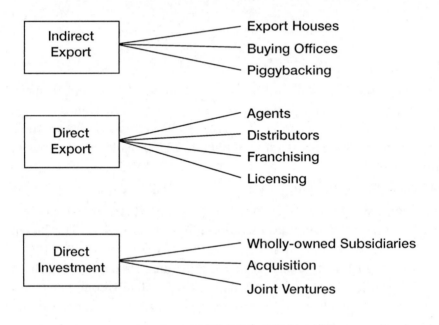

Figure 13.5 Foreign Market Entry Alternatives

Figure 13.5 details the options available within each foreign market entry method. For a company wishing to market its goods internationally, the entry decision is a crucial one. The entry method that is selected affects the operations and success of a company. Indeed, many companies begin international marketing though indirect export and, over the longer term, change to more direct methods. It may be tempting to select the simplest form of entry but, for a company with a longer-term view, various criteria should be considered:

Cost: perhaps the lowest-cost entry method is indirect exporting. It requires little financial, manpower or time investment.

Risk: indirect exporting involves a limited amount of financial risk. However, because of the limited control experienced by the manufacturer, it may be risky in terms of image. Direct investment is the riskiest entry strategy because of the level of resource required.

Company capability: a company with limited resources and knowledge might consider indirect exporting initially. A company with available resources may consider direct exporting or direct investment.

Payback period: direct investment involves long payback periods. It could be several years before money is recuperated.

Knowledge: if a company has limited knowledge of international markets it can gain immediate know-how through the use of direct exporting methods via agents and distributors.

Type of product: perishable products require more direct entry methods. Technical products may require servicing and spare parts and so direct exporting or direct investment are preferred.

Strategy: if a company intends to expand into more countries, direct exporting and direct investment may be favoured.

Control: indirect exporting offers the manufacturer limited control over the elements of the marketing mix. A direct exporting method such as franchising offers more control. Direct investment offers the highest levels of control.

Environment: some countries are only accessible through joint ventures, because of legal requirements.

Stage 4: How Should we Manage the Marketing Mix?

Once a company has decided on its market entry strategy, it can begin to consider the marketing mix. You should note that this may not be appropriate for indirect exporting where limited amounts of control exist.

The elements of the marketing mix are the same in both domestic and international marketing. The major decision to be taken is whether to standardise or adapt the marketing mix for international markets.

Standardisation means that a similar marketing mix is used internationally. In other words the same products are sold under the same brand names at the same price using the same promotions all over the world. Coca-Cola, McDonald's and Burger King pursue a standardisation strategy. This is often known as a globalisation strategy where similar segments are sought around the world and satisfied with similar marketing mixes. A company that pursues a global, standardised strategy benefits from economies of scale in production and promotion as well as global recognition.

Adaptation means that the marketing mix is changed or adapted for each country or market that the product is sold in. Procter and Gamble and Unilever pursue a strategy of adaptation. The basis of this strategy is that customers all over the world have different needs and wants. In order to satisfy these different needs and wants, companies modify the marketing mix to suit individual markets. In this way, customers can be better satisfied.

The standardisation and adaptation debate has continued for years. Levitt (1983) is perhaps the most recognised author on this subject. He emphasized the importance of global products and brands as the key to success for international companies. Other authors have argued that full standardisation is impossible to achieve internationally because of different laws, economies and cultures throughout the world.

Certainly there are macro forces that encourage global standardisation:

◆ **Market homogeneity:** customer needs and wants are becoming increasingly similar worldwide. This is perhaps driven by improved global communications where customers everywhere are aware of the types of products and services that exist.

◆ **Country of origin appeal:** some products are attractive internationally because of their origin. For example Scotch Whisky, Irish Linen and Belgian Chocolate are more attractive because of their origin.

◆ **Consumer mobility:** we travel more than ever before. Because of increased levels of travel consumers are becoming more aware of international products.

These factors do drive globalisation but there are many factors that encourage adaptation. Figure 13.6 provides an overview of the factors that encourage marketing mix adaptation. You can see from this figure that achieving total standardisation of the marketing mix is difficult.

Mix Macro Factors	Product	Price	Place	Promotion
Politics/legal	◆ Product regulations differ throughout the world	◆ Some governments enforce price controls ◆ Tariffs affect costs	◆ Joint ventures are enforced in some countries	◆ Advertising and media restrictions may exist
Economic	◆ Lower disposable income may force changes in product	◆ Lower disposable income may force price reductions ◆ Exchange rate fluctuations may affect pricing	◆ Physical distribution may change because of transportation available	◆ Limited amount of media availability in less developed countries
Social	◆ Different customer tastes and habits	◆ Negotiation is common in many countries	◆ Different buying behaviour ◆ Differing demographics	◆ Language and attitude differences ◆ Lower customer literacy levels
Technological	◆ Electricity may be unavailable ◆ Different local power supply ◆ Lower customer technical skills	◆ EPOS systems may not exist	◆ Direct marketing via the internet may be impossible ◆ Poor standards of maintenance	◆ Advertising media may be unavailable

Figure 13.6 Factors Encouraging Adaptation of the Marketing Mix Internationally

Once the standardisation/adaptation decision is taken, a company can begin to manage and design its marketing mix for international markets. As with all marketing strategy it will be necessary to monitor and evaluate the success of all decisions that have been taken.

Summary

This chapter has introduced the complexities involved in international marketing. It may be profitable for a company to sell its goods overseas but careful planning is advised. A four-stage process is recommended: Should we market overseas? Which countries shall we sell to? What market entry method should we use? How should we manage the marketing mix?

The decision to market overseas affects the rest of a company's operations. Selling internationally offers the chance to increase profits, spread risk and achieve economies of scale. However, substantial investment may be required if international marketing is to be successful.

If a company decides to expand internationally, it should decide on the countries it will enter. A screening process is recommended to eliminate countries that have little market potential.

There are three options for market entry: indirect exporting, direct exporting and direct investment. Selecting the entry method depends on many factors including cost, risk, payback period, the product and company capability.

The major marketing mix decision when selling goods internationally is concerned with standardisation or adaptation. Standardisation involves selling similar products at similar prices using similar promotions worldwide. Adaptation means changing or modifying elements of the marketing mix to suit local culture and tastes.

Review Questions

1. List five reasons why a company may decide to pursue an international marketing strategy.

2. What are the stages of the screening process when deciding which countries to enter?

3. Explain tariff and non-tariff barriers.

4. What is the purpose of protectionism?

5. Why do governments encourage exporting?

6. List three sources of international secondary information.

7. Why is it advisable to use an agency when performing international primary research?

8. What are the three main market entry methods?

9. Identify two advantages and two disadvantages of franchising as an international entry method.

10. Identify and explain five criteria that a company may consider making the market entry decision.

11. Explain the concept of globalisation.

12. List five factors that might encourage adaptation of the marketing mix.

Discussion Questions

1. 'Consumer tastes are the same all over the world'. Discuss.

2. Explain why standardisation of the marketing mix may be difficult to achieve internationally.

3. Why is acquisition used in preference to wholly-owned subsidiaries as a market entry method?

4. Identify and discuss the macro factors that encourage a company to expand into international markets.

5. Explain how protectionism impacts on world trade.

Key Terms

Acquisition	Distributors	Joint venture
Adaptation	Entry method	Licensing
Agents	EU	Non-tariff
Buying offices	Export houses	Piggybacking
Culture	Franchising	Standardisation
Direct exporting	Globalisation	Tariff
Direct investment	Indirect exporting	Wholly-owned subsidiaries

Chapter 14
Relationship Marketing and Internal Marketing

Introduction

Throughout this book the terms 'relationship marketing' and 'internal marketing' have been mentioned. We will now look at these areas of marketing in more depth. We will deal with relationship marketing and introduce the concept of internal marketing later in the chapter (although it has been discussed in Chapter 12 at some length).

As its name suggests, relationship marketing is about building relationships. You have perhaps assumed that the term implies building relationships with customers – and, yes, this is correct. However, it is too narrow a definition. Gummesson (1999) defines it as '....marketing seen as relationships, networks and interaction'.

Therefore, it is more than building a relationship with customers. It is building a whole network of relationships with parties or organisations that are key to the success of a company. Figure 14.1 indicates the parties and organisations that are key to relationship marketing. The parties/organisations are known as markets. In building a relationship marketing programme, a company should consider each of these markets.

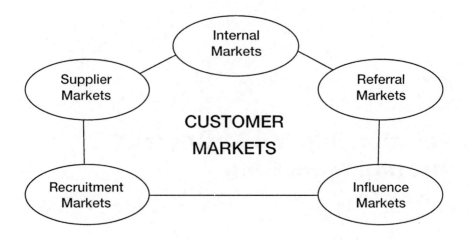

Figure 14.1 The Six Markets Model (Peck et al 1999)

Customer Markets

This book has concentrated on the activities that a marketer might perform to achieve customer satisfaction and build relationships with customers. In fact, the whole or the strategic marketing process (see Chapter 2) is concerned with customer satisfaction. Thus, the purpose of marketing research, target marketing and the marketing mix is to achieve customer satisfaction. A satisfied customer may become loyal to a company and we already know that it is less expensive to retain customers than to find new ones. So, relationship marketing focuses on repeat buying rather than one-off transactions. This is illustrated in the loyalty ladder displayed in Figure 14.2.

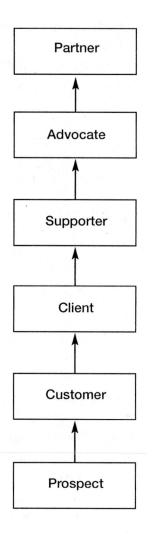

Figure 14.2 The Loyalty Ladder (Christopher et al 1991)

The lowest rung of the ladder is the contact with a *prospect* who hopefully turns into a *customer* by making a first purchase. Those customers that return to a company and make repeated purchases are known as *clients*. Although a relationship is beginning, clients are likely to be neutral about a company rather than keen supporters. A *supporter* is someone who actually likes the company. A company that can turn supporters into *advocates* benefit from strong word-of-mouth because advocates are likely to recommend and refer the company to their friends and colleagues. The final stage is that of a *partner*. Here, the company actually builds up a relationship with the customer.

You should realise that a customer can be defined in many ways. The following identifies various types of customers:

◆ **Consumers:** these are the individuals at the end of a channel who buy products and services.

◆ **Intermediaries:** these are the members of the distribution channels. They are also customers.

◆ **Business buyers:** companies that buy products for business or industrial use are also customers.

The importance of each of these customer groups will vary according to the company that is selling products or services. For instance, the consumer will be of high importance to a retailer. A wholesaler may be extremely important to a manufacturer of consumer goods, but this same manufacturer must also attempt to satisfy the consumer. A business buyer is an important customer for a business-to-business company.

The marketing techniques that have been discussed throughout this book can be used effectively to build relationships with any type of customer group. Recently, companies have attempted to learn more about their customers through constant information gathering. Supermarkets gain information about consumers through loyalty cards. Direct marketing companies gain information about customers through data gathering on their internet sites. Information about customers provides companies with the means to better satisfy their needs.

Supplier Markets

Suppliers are vital to the success of a company. Without a constant source of supply, a company cannot hope to satisfy its own customers. Therefore, building relationships with suppliers may be valuable – especially if the bargaining power of suppliers is high (Moore, 1999). Refer to Chapter 3 for an overview of the conditions that create high supplier bargaining power.

Many companies do not realise the benefits of building relationships or partnerships with suppliers. In Chapter 10 of this book we discussed the concept of Vertical Marketing Systems (VMS). One type of VMS is the administered VMS where one member of a distribution channel exerts its power over other channel members. Relationship marketing is more concerned with building and sustaining partnerships with the suppliers than dominating them.

A partnership means that both parties benefit from the relationship. There are many benefits for a company that builds relationships with suppliers including:

- ◆ **Cost reductions:** because the supplier understands the needs of the buying company. Also, costly mistakes will decrease because of this understanding.

- ◆ **New product development:** the supplier can become involved in NPD. It may be a valuable source of new product ideas.

- ◆ **Information sharing:** the buying company may gain valuable information from a supplier about markets, new products and competitors.

- ◆ **Improved performance:** the supplier should improve performance throughout the relationship because of increased knowledge of the buying organisation.

- ◆ **Motivation:** because the supplier is gaining from the relationship, he will be motivated to perform better.

- ◆ **Assured source of supply:** relationships are valuable, particularly in markets where supplier bargaining power is high.

- ◆ **Competitive advantage:** a relationship may help the buying company to gain competitive advantage if competitors have sourcing difficulties.

We have looked at the benefits of a relationship from the buying company's point of view. These benefits can also be applied to the supplier. It is not suggested that a company can build relationships effectively with all suppliers. It is recommended that relationships are developed with key suppliers. If this relationship strategy is to be pursued, selection of suppliers becomes a vital issue.

Referral Markets

A referral market consists of those parties that refer or recommend a company to friends, family and colleagues. We already know that a 'word-of-mouth' recommendation is one of the best forms of marketing that exists.

Chapters 5 and 6 of this book discussed the concept of buyer behaviour. In consumer buying behaviour reference groups have a significant impact on the buying decision. Family, friends, colleagues, religious groups, trade unions, etc may have a direct influence during the information search stage of the decision-making process. A company that receives positive recommendations or referrals from these reference groups may achieve increased sales levels. Many consumer companies are beginning to realise the importance of reference groups. They realise that their customers are also members of reference groups and therefore actively encourage positive recommendations. For instance, The Britannia Music Club gives free CDs to customers who recommend the company to family and friends. This is much less a form of promotion than advertising or direct marketing.

In business-to-business markets the buyer can be influenced by any member of the decision-making unit. Again, a company may seek to gain positive recommendations from the decision-making unit members. This means that a company should seek to build relationships with all members of the decision-making unit – not just the buyers.

Influence Markets

This market consists of the publics of an organisation including banks, pressure groups, the local community, and the general public. The opinion and feeling of a company's public may have a direct impact on its success.

Many companies attempt to build relationships with publics through effective public relations campaigns. They realise that negative publicity can be damaging and so attempt to generate positive publicity. Think about the publicity generated by Channel 4's Big Brother programme. Audience figures almost doubled over a five week period because of the amount of publicity the programme has generated. Effective public relations campaigns are essential. For further information on public relations, you should refer to Chapter 11 of this book.

Recruitment Markets

High calibre and motivated staff are essential to a company that wishes to pursue a relationship marketing programme. It is through employees that relationships are established with supplier, referral, influence and supplier markets. Therefore, effective recruitment is essential.

The recruitment market consists of potential employees and any other parties involved in recruiting them (agencies, consultancies, universities, etc). The purpose of relationship marketing in this area is to ensure that the 'best' people actually apply for vacant positions. From the applicants the 'best' person should be selected and then trained to fill the position.

The image of a company is important in actually encouraging people to apply for jobs at a company. Therefore, the referral and influence markets have a direct impact on the quality of people that apply to a company. The first stage of relationship marketing in recruitment markets is to attract applications.

To deal with applications effectively, a company should have an established selection procedure. The purpose of selection is to ensure that the 'best' or most suitable person gets the job. Or, from another viewpoint, that those applicants with limited potential are eliminated as early as possible from the selection procedure. Remember, it is vital to ensure that suitable employees are recruited because they deal directly with all other markets. Once recruited, employees should receive adequate training to ensure that they can do the job effectively.

Recruitment is expensive. If the recruitment and selection process fails (the wrong candidate is selected), cost is increased. Investment is needed by many companies in this area.

Internal Markets

Internal markets consist of staff – those that have been recruited. This is an area that has been much debated in the sphere of marketing. It relates to the way employees are treated within a company. Good internal marketing results in happy, motivated employees that perform well. People are particularly important in services marketing but more and more product companies are realising the importance of staff in achieving customer satisfaction. For a fuller discussion of internal marketing you should refer to Chapter 12 of this book.

Summary

So, you can see that relationship marketing involves building relationships with a network of markets. These relationships should evolve and develop over time. It is commonly assumed that relationship marketing involves building relationships with customers. Although customers are an important aspect of relationship marketing, it is key that relationships are also established with supplier markets, referral markets, influence markets, recruitment markets and internal markets.

Suppliers are important to a company that is seeking to satisfy its customers. A high quality, continual source of supply is more likely if relationships are built with suppliers. The added benefit of this is reduced costs, greater information flow and competitive advantage.

Word-of-mouth is one of the most effective promotional tools. It is inexpensive and credible. Therefore, building relationships with referral markets is essential to ensure positive recommendations for a company.

Influence markets are formed by the publics of an organisation. It is important to build a relationship with influencers so that a favourable image of a company is generated.

It is essential a company recruits high calibre staff and is able to retain them through effective internal marketing programmes. It is staff who deal with all the other relationship markets. Without their cooperation and commitment a company cannot hope to be successful in the longer term.

Review Questions

1. What is relationship marketing?
2. List five benefits of a relationship marketing programme.
3. What are the key markets in relationship marketing?
4. What are the steps in the relationship ladder? Explain each stage.
5. Why are supplier relationships important?
6. List three benefits of effective supplier relationships.
7. What is the referral market?
8. Who are a company's publics and why are they important in relationship marketing?
9. Why are staff so important in relationship marketing?
10. List five methods that might be used to motivate staff.

Discussion Questions

1. 'The costs of relationship marketing far outweigh the benefits'. Discuss.
2. 'Internal marketing is another name for HRM'. Discuss.
3. How might the sales team contribute to an effective relationship marketing programme?

4. What methods might each of the following companies use to encourage positive referrals from their customers:

    - A car dealer?

    - A computer software company?

    - A retailer?

Key Terms

Advocate	Internal markets	Relationship ladder
Client	Partner	Relationship marketing
Customer	Prospect	Supplier markets
Customer markets	Recruitment markets	Supporter
Influence markets	Referral markets	

References

Adcock D, Bradfield R, Halborg A and Ross C (1995) *Marketing Principles & Practice*, Second Edition, Pitman Publishing.

Armstrong, G and Kotler, P (1987) *Marketing An Introduction.* Prentice Hall.

Berry L L (1995) On Great Service, *A Framework for Action,* Free Press, New York.

Berry L L and Parasuraman, A (1991) *Marketing Services: Competing through Quality,* Free Press, New York.

Bickerton P, Beickerton M and Pardesi U (1996) *Cybermarketing,* Butterworth Heinemann.

Bonoma and Shaprio (1983) *Segmenting the Industrial Market,* Lexington Books.

Bradley F (1991) *International Marketing Strategy,* Prentice Hall.

Cahill D J (1996) *Internal Marketing Your Company's Next Stage of Growth,* The Haworth Press, Inc.

Chee H and Harris R (1993) *Marketing A Global Perspective,* Pitman Publishing.

Chisnall P M (1992) *Marketing Research,* McGraw Hill.

Chisnall P M (1995) *Strategic Business Marketing,* 3rd Edition, Prentice Hall.

Christopher M, Payne A and Ballantyne D (1991) *Relationship Marketing,* Butterworth Heinemann, Oxford.

Cole G A, (1996) *Management Theory and Practice,* 5th Edition, Letts. 1996.

Cowell D (1984) *The Marketing of Services,* Heinemann.

Dibb S, Simkin L, Pride W M and Ferrell O C (1997) *Marketing,* The European Edition, Houghton Mifflin.

Doole I, Lowe R and Phillips C (1994) *International Marketing Strategy,* Thomson Business Press.

Drucker P (1977) *People and Performance,* Butterworth Heinemann.

Ewing M T and Caruana A (1999) 'An internal marketing approach to public sector management, the marketing and human resources interface', *The International Journal of Public Sector Management* 12 (1). 17-26.

Gummesson E (1999) *Total Relationship Marketing*, Butterworth Heinemann.

Hall E T (1976) *Beyond Culture*, New York, Doubleday.

Hasty R and Reardon J (1997) *Retail Management*, The McGraw-Hill Companies, Inc.

Hill E and O'Sullivan, T (1996) *Marketing*, Longman.

Hutt M D and Speh T W (1992) *Business Marketing Management*, Dryden.

Johannsen H and Page G T *International Dictionary of Management*, Kogan Page.

Keegan W J (1989) *Global Marketing Management*, Prentice Hall International Editions.

Kotler P (2000) *Marketing Management*, The Millennium Edition, Prentice Hall.

Lancaster G and Reynolds P (1995) *Marketing*, Butterworth Heinemann.

Levitt T (1960) 'Marketing Myopia', *Harvard Business Review*, July-August, pp 45-56.

Levitt T (1983) 'The Globalization of Markets', *Harvard Business Review*, May-June, pp 92-102.

Lings N I (1999) 'Balancing Internal and External Market Orientations', *Journal of Marketing Management* 15, pp 239-263.

Lovelock C (1992) *Managing Services*, Prentice Hall.

Lynch R (1997) *Corporate Strategy*, Pitman Publishing.

Mazur L (1999) 'Unleashing employee' true value; employees can be your company's most valuable marketing asset', *Marketing*, April 29 pp22.

McDonald M (1999) *Marketing Plans*, Butterworth Heinemann.

Mercer D (1992) *Marketing*, Blackwell Business.

Moore M (1999) *Commercial Relationships*, Tudor Publishing.

Paliwoda S J and Thomas M J (1998) *International Marketing*, 3rd Edition, Butterworth Heinemann.

Peck H, Payne A, Christopher M and Clark M (1999) *Relationship Marketing Strategy and Implementation*, Butterworth Heinemann

Pervais K A and Rafiq M (1995) 'The role of internal marketing in the implementation of marketing strategies' , *Journal of Marketing Practice* 1(4), pp 32-51.

Schiffman L G and Kanuk L L (2000) *Consumer Behaviour*, 7th Edition, Prentice Hall.

Schultz D E (24/5/99) 'Perhaps the 4Ps really should be the 4Rs', *Marketing News*.

Seithaml V, Parasauraman A and Berry L (1985) 'Problems and strategies in services marketing', *Journal of Marketing*, Spring, pp 33-46.

Sweet Facts (1999) The Annual Review of the Confectionery Market.

Smith I (1994) *Meeting Customer Needs*, Butterworth Heinemann.

Index

Chartered Institute of Marketing (CIM) 2

Clinique 90

Coca-Cola 18, 32, 34, 125, 129, 149, 171, 179, 188-9, 192

Competitors 30-3, 116

Competitive bidding 123

Competitive rivalry 31 *et seq*

Consumer buying behaviour Ch 5 *passim*, 65

- buying process 62-3

- cognititive dissonance 56, 65

- consumer ch 5 *passim*, 65

- culture 57-8, 65

- customer Ch 5 *passim*, 65

- decision making 54, 57, 62-3, 65

- economic situation 60

- end user 62, 63

- evaluation 55-6

- influences 57 *et seq*

- lifecycle 59-60, 65

- lifestyle 61, 65

- motivation 55, 56, 65

- need recogninition 54, 55

- perception 55, 65

- personality 57, 59, 61, 65

- psychological influcences 61, 65

- reference groups 58, 65

- social class 58, 65

- social environment 57-8, 65

- socio-economic grouping 59, 65

- SPADE 62-3, 65

Control process 19-20

Corporate objectives 10, 12, 115

Customer 8, 29-30, 37, Ch5 *passim*, 199, 206

- needs and wants 6-7

- satisfaction 8

D

Daewoo 130, 158

Dell Computers 158

Demand 114-5, 123, *see also price*

Demographics 70, 80, 87, 187, *see also market research*

Department for Trade and Industry(DTI) 24

Discounts 119, 123

Disney 188

Distribution 116, *see also place*

Dixons 143

Duke's Transport 81

E

Economic pricing 123, *see also price*

Environment, marketing 12 *et seq*

Printed in the United Kingdom
by Lightning Source UK Ltd.
2156

9 781903 500033